the Coaching handbook

An action kit for trainers & managers

Sara Thorpe & Jackie Clifford

KOGAN PAGE

London and Sterling, VA

First published in Great Britain and the United States in 2003 by Kogan Page Limited

120 Pentonville Road
London N1 9JN
UK
www.kogan-page.co.uk

22883 Quicksilver Drive
Sterling VA 20166-2012
USA

ISBN 0 7494 3810 X

British Library Cataloguing-in-Publication Data

A CIP record for this book is available from the British Library

Typeset by JS Typesetting Ltd, Wellingborough, Northants
Printed and bound in Great Britain by Clays Ltd, St Ives plc

Contents

Part 3: Activities and exercises 175

Map your journey; Highs and lows; Spider charts; Force field analysis; Guided imagery; Unfinished sentences; Tuning in to body language; Move your watch; Give it back; Skills checklist; SWOT analysis; 'What if...' questions; Best in the world; Cats and refrigerators; Evaluating progress; Review technique; My frustration journal; Positive affirmation; Personality strengths; Edward de Bono's six thinking hats; Reframing; Using research; Questions, questions, questions; A problem-solving process; Questionnaires; Demonstrations; Role-play; Case study; In-tray exercises

Acknowledgements

We would like to thank all those around us who have supported us as we wrote this book. Special thanks go to Geoff, George, Majid, Claire and Peter for their patience, especially in the latter stages. We would also like to say 'thank you' to all those who contributed the case studies in Part 2.

Introduction

Everyone is talking about coaching. As people who work within the field of learning and development, we find that we are constantly asked for training in coaching skills and to help organizations introduce coaching schemes. Line managers are told that an important part of their role is coaching. Trainers are increasingly asked to coach individuals.

In researching background material for training courses we have found that much of the training and reading material available focuses on the *skills* of a coach – the art of active listening, asking questions, and summarizing action points. Whilst the skills are essential, there seems to be a lack of an agreed process – as a coach, at what point do I use which skills? Where do I start when asked to coach a colleague? How long will it take? What methods do I employ?

When we started discussing coaching, we discovered that we both had different views of what it is and how it takes place. We had originally assumed that, having worked together for some years, we automatically meant the same thing by the words we were using! The differences were not immense, but were sufficient to make us question and probe further into defining the whole subject area. Having reviewed coaching within a number of organizations, read a number of books and talked to various different line managers and trainers, we realized that we were not alone in our different understandings of coaching. Definitions of the term 'coaching' that we have come across range from on-the-job training to performance management discussions.

In this book the definition of coaching we have used is:

*The process of helping someone **enhance** or **improve** their performance through reflection on how they apply a specific skill and/or knowledge.*

Chapter 1 discusses in depth this definition and how it relates to the fundamental principles of learning. It also gives you the opportunity to think about the similarities and differences between coaching and training, mentoring, counselling and line management.

Our aim in writing this book is to provide you with a straightforward and practical process for coaching others. We hope that it will help demystify the coaching process so that you have a structure to use regardless of the situation or your past experience with coaching. It is about giving you the confidence to coach others without feeling that you need to be a 'qualified' coach to do it. Whether you have attended formal training in coaching or not, our purpose in writing the book is to provide readily available hints and tips for you to access as and when you need them.

The model of coaching that we offer is based upon our own experiences as we have developed from classroom trainers into line managers for whom coaching is an essential part of the role. At the same time as we were making this personal transition we found ourselves working more with our client groups to assist in implementing coaching programmes and providing coaching for individuals outside our teams. We have built a model that we believe to be flexible and easy to use; we make no apologies for our practical, rather than academic, approach to the topic.

This book is divided into three parts (read it from cover to cover, or dip in and out, whichever suits your own learning style):

- Part 1. Along with the definition of coaching, you will find a practical model of coaching here. Each stage of the model is discussed in detail with tips for helping you implement it, thoughts around the skills required at each stage and ideas to use if things don't go quite as you had planned.
- Part 2. This gives a series of case studies from people who have coached or been coached in their professional, sporting or personal life.
- Part 3. Here you will find a range of activities and exercises for you to adapt and use in your coaching sessions.

The book also contains a Further Reading section that lists useful publications for your reference as you develop in your coaching role.

We hope that you enjoy using this book. We would welcome your feedback and would like to hear about your personal coaching experiences. Contact us on deartrainer@btopenworld.com

Sara and Jackie

Part 1

The coaching process

1

What is coaching?

We define coaching as:

*The process of helping people **enhance** or **improve** their performance through reflection on how they apply a specific skill and/or knowledge.*

Coaching is about developing individuals beyond where they currently are. Before we say more about what coaching is, perhaps we should say something about development in general terms.

Development is fundamental to the survival of both the individual and the organization; it is to the business world the same as evolution is to the biological world. Few companies have a business plan which aims to make their organization extinct or less competitive and successful. All individuals need to adapt to the rapidly changing, and increasingly complex world in which we live – whether they adapt by opting out or by embracing newness.

Development is defined as:

A continuous process of growing and learning; by developing, we continuously become more than we were.

Development is about gaining new knowledge, skills and behaviours; or about adapting the ones we have (ie learning). It is, therefore, about change. Change is something that happens to everybody but that does not stop it being difficult and stressful, even at times painful. In her book *Message from Forever*, Marlo Morgan says, 'Life is change. Some big, some little, but without change there can be no growing. And change and growth do not imply either pain or sacrifice.'

Coaching is one tool that can be used to help others develop. It is, therefore, about supporting the change process and, used effectively, coaching should help lessen the impact of change and maximize the opportunities for growth.

Change is a cyclical process. As a coach it is useful for you to be aware of the cycle, which describes our natural response to change, so that you can help your coachees to move through the cycle.

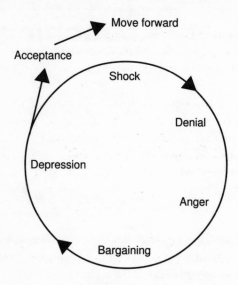

Figure 1.1 The cycle of change, as described by a number of authors including Elisabeth Kübler-Ross. It is important to recognize that individuals need to move through all stages, to acceptance, before they can move on

Development needs

We define a development need as:

The difference between current and required (or desired) performance.

Identifying a development need involves being clear about what your start point is and what the desired end point is going to be.

Development needs can be met in a number of ways – coaching is one of them – we will talk shortly about the correlation between coaching and other development activities such as line management, training and counselling.

Development – core values and beliefs

Given that coaching is about development, we believe that successful coaches are people who believe the following:

- All people are capable of development.
- People can only change if they want to and are ready to.
- What others believe about our potential can influence the level of our success.
- What we believe about our own potential is directly linked to our success.
- How we define success will have a direct impact upon what we achieve.
- We limit our potential by having limiting beliefs, eg believing that certain things are not possible due to environmental or situational constraints.
- People will only learn when they are truly engaged with the process.
- It is possible to learn from everything that we do, but learning only happens when we reflect and plan for next time (see Kolb's learning theory in Chapter 2).
- People don't need to be experts before they can help someone learn – in fact sometimes it is better if they are not as they will not be stuck in the 'right way' of doing things.
- In order to help others develop, we must continue to develop ourselves.

Training

One development tool that is often confused with coaching is training.

Training is the process by which someone learns a new skill or piece of knowledge. It is giving someone the tools to do a job, thereby moving that person from conscious incompetence to conscious competence (see Chapter 2). At the end of a training session the learner may be able to do the job, but not necessarily achieve the required standard all of the time. Training can be formal (eg training courses) or informal (such as on-the-job instruction).

True learning does not take place until the learner has transferred it from the training environment into the 'real world', and made a persistent change in behaviour.

This is where coaching comes in. Coaching takes place either when a person is consciously competent or unconsciously competent, but needs to move his or her performance to the next level.

It is worth noting that sometimes learners will describe themselves as being consciously incompetent, where in reality they have the skills and/or knowledge required to undertake the task, but they have not used them in this particular way. In this situation we believe that there will not necessarily be a requirement for training and that coaching will support individuals in transferring their skills into another setting. This is an excellent example of why it is so important to get to know your learner prior to coaching.

Coaching helps people to reflect on their performance in a specific area with an informed, objective helper. It is about helping individuals to implement their learning within the workplace and therefore improve their performance. It is not about teaching something new. The prime focus of coaching should be on using existing knowledge and skills, perhaps reviewing attitude and approach, to maximize performance.

Many trainers struggle to define the difference between coaching and training – some because they like to think that training has a bigger impact on performance than it has; others because their style is more facilitative and they incorporate coaching within their sessions.

Figure 1.2 The continuum of development

We believe that training and coaching will often overlap. Sometimes when coaching someone, it may become apparent that he or she does not have the necessary skills or background knowledge; at this point, the coaching stops and training begins. Training and coaching are part of the continuum of development.

It is possible, therefore, that within a person's role there will be many coaching experiences – potentially for as many skills as are required for that position (see Figure 1.3). An effective personal development plan (PDP) will prioritize the skills that need working on at any particular time in order to ensure that the individual is fulfilling his or her potential and achieving business objectives.

Coaching is fundamentally a relationship between two people that exists for a given purpose; once that purpose has been achieved, that relationship is no longer required. The purpose? To help individuals move from where they are to where they want or need to be – to develop them.

Let's look at some other terms that are linked to and confused with coaching.

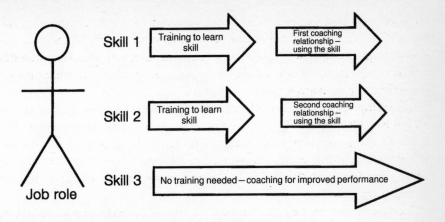

Figure 1.3 The relationship of coaching with training: how an individual might develop different skills for a job

Mentoring

Many organizations couple coaching and mentoring together as part of the same scheme or process. Again, we would agree that there is an element of overlapping; but for the purpose of this book, we have excluded mentoring. We define mentoring as:

General guidance or advice regarding life or career.

Mentoring, which covers a range of issues, is much more general than coaching, which looks at a specific skill or area. It usually helps people progress within a specific field or organization and helps individuals look at how they use their networking, profile and organizational politics.

More often than not a mentor is someone who is senior to their mentee, either within the organization or within their specialist field. In seeking a mentor, individuals will look for a role model who they can relate to on a personal level as well as someone who is well-respected within their area. This differs from coaching in a number of ways:

- The coach does not have to be senior to their coachee.
- The relationship is not so personal – the coachee does not need to like his or her coach, but a mentee generally needs to like his or her mentor.
- Coaching is about one specific subject, where mentoring is about general issues of career and life development.

Counselling

We mention counselling because it uses similar skills to coaching. A counsellor will generally be used by individuals to help them deal with a specific problem; counselling focuses on emotions and feelings rather than performance. Counselling tends to look at the causes for today's issues; it looks at the past and the route taken to arrive at the point where the individual currently is. Coaching turns the attention to the future, with the starting point being where the individual is today; its focus is on planning a route to arrive at a pre-agreed point.

Within the workplace, individuals would generally only seek the advice of a counsellor if they had a problem, whereas coaching can involve the development of good performance as well as under-performance.

Line management

Line management is the art of getting the best out of people to achieve an objective and therefore an effective line manager may employ the other roles outlined above as appropriate to the situation. Much has been written about the role of the line manager in coaching. Current thinking seems to suggest that an effective line manager will coach his or her team members as and when this is required. We think that what line managers are actually being asked to adopt is a coaching *style*, rather than necessarily do the coaching. A coaching style is one where individual development is encouraged, through whichever means is appropriate for that individual, team and organization – it is a style which is able to adapt and be flexible to changing needs. An effective manager, therefore, is one who recognizes that a development need exists and knows whether or not he or she is the right person to conduct the coaching (when coaching is chosen to fulfil the need). If that manager is not the right person, he or she may choose someone else in the team or organization or look externally for a coach.

Indicators that the line manager will not be an effective coach are:

- There is not a good relationship between the line manager and the individual.
- Relationships within the organization are formal and laid down by procedure and hierarchy.
- The line manager is still developing his or her coaching skills and the situation does not lend itself to being used for 'practising'.

- The work of the department would make it difficult for both coach and coachee to allocate time to the coaching.
- The coachee would value or benefit from third party involvement.

A key fault with some coaching schemes is that they ask line managers to become coaches without first checking whether these individuals believe in, and understand, development.

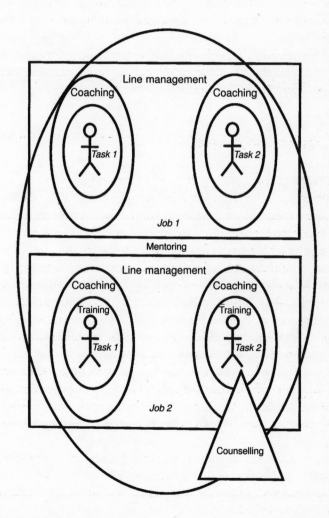

Figure 1.4 The relationship of coaching to training, mentoring, counselling and line management

Benefits of coaching

Coaching is a person-centred activity; working with individuals in this way makes them feel valued which has an immediate effect upon their motivation and therefore their performance. Addressing individual needs means that budgets can be allocated more specifically and outcomes can be more readily measured. Coaching is a flexible approach – it can be used within organizations and environments where it is not generally possible to take whole groups of staff away for off-the-job, formal training. Equally, it can be used to address one-off needs as and when they arise. The organization therefore gets performance-related development in a more cost-effective and flexible way. Individuals gain practical and realistic help to achieve their full potential and work on their areas of weakness – they get targeted, practical development from coaching, where training tends to be broader and looser and requires follow-up within the workplace if it is to be effective.

Summary

- Coaching is the process of enhancing or improving skills and/or knowledge in a specific area.
- It is a one-to-one activity.
- Coaching could take place on the job or in a separate setting.
- Each cycle of coaching is about applying the skills and knowledge already learnt to a specific situation or purpose. The learning of those skills and knowledge may have taken place recently, or some time previously; it may be the result of a formal training or informal experience.
- Successful coaching will result in an improvement in performance, as its ultimate aim is to help someone to transfer his or her learning.
- A person will never be coached unless the skill or knowledge is to be used in the near future.
- The coach needs to know what the skill or knowledge will look like when it is being implemented and have the skill or knowledge at a certain level – the coach does not necessarily need to be able to perform the skill or knowledge at the level required by the coachee.

2

Learning theories

In this chapter, we have collated some of the theories that underpin current thinking on learning and development. You may be familiar with these; however, we include them as a reminder, or for those of you who have not been exposed to them previously.

Theory of competence

This theory states that learning is a four-stage process, which involves the journey from unconscious incompetence to unconscious competence.

Unconscious incompetence

This is where you are unaware that you do not know something or cannot do it – it is the 'I don't know what I don't know' level. There is probably little need or requirement for you to have the skill or knowledge in question and this is why you have not yet developed the awareness of your lack of competence. For example, as a very young child in a car you will have been aware of travelling from one place to another in the car, but may not have realized that you didn't know how to drive – so were unaware of the inability.

Conscious incompetence

This is where you become aware of your lack of capability, usually because a need or desire to do something has arisen. This is the stage of 'I know what I don't know'. Back to our example – as a teenager who can't drive you become aware of constantly asking for lifts to get to places and are acutely aware of your inability to drive.

Conscious competence

To become consciously competent, you will go through some form of learning – either formal or informal. Often at this stage you will do things in exactly the way you have been shown how to do them (subject to your memory). You are aware at every moment of what you are doing – you 'know what you know'. Back to the driving example – say, for example, that at 17 you have driving lessons and duly pass your test; for a while you will still be thinking 'mirror, signal and manoeuvre' – you have to think about how to drive.

Unconscious competence

This is where your knowledge and skills have been used so often they are 'habits'– you don't need to think about the next part of the process to carry it out, as it is stored in the unconscious (or subconscious) part of your brain. It is the 'I don't know what I know'. When you have been driving for a few years it will have become second nature. Say, for example, you try to teach your child to drive – you are unaware of the detail of what you do when you drive as it is ingrained behaviour.

Kolb's learning cycle

Kolb stated that for true learning to take place, we need to have an experience, reflect upon this experience, make sense of it (often through creating theories) and finally apply our theories to our lives by planning what we would do next time we were in the same or similar situation.

In order to learn from an experience, you have to go through the learning cycle; sometimes you may do this unconsciously. Formal development processes (training, coaching, mentoring, self-study etc) involve bringing all four stages into consciousness and ensuring that the process of learning is completed. Learning is inhibited when one of Kolb's stages is missed.

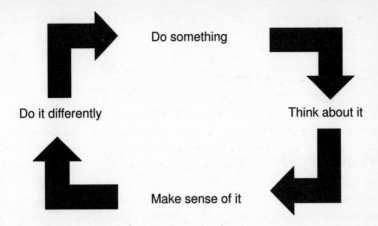

Figure 2.1 Kolb's learning cycle

Honey and Mumford's learning styles

Honey and Mumford identified four styles of learning preference, which map onto Kolb's learning cycle:

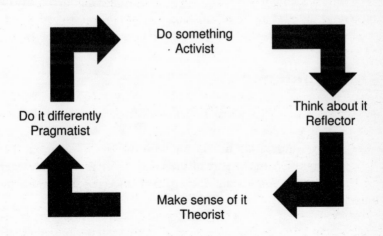

Figure 2.2 Kolb's learning cycle with Honey and Mumford's learning styles

People with a strong preference as described by Honey and Mumford are more likely to want to miss out, or stay within, one of the stages. For example: a strong activist likes to try experience after experience and will try to avoid reflection or theorizing. Therefore, the role of the development specialist working with a learner is to ensure that all stages are addressed in a way which is easiest for the individual.

Often, to make a major change, we might go around the circle more than once. This is the only way of ensuring that we get the practice required for behaviour to become a habit. As we discuss later, this is particularly important in coaching.

Barriers to learning

Having described how learning takes place, it is worth considering that there are some barriers which may get in the way of an individual's learning.

Previous experience

An individual who has had a bad learning experience either at school or on a training course or who has been embarrassed by a line manager or colleague may be nervous about entering the coaching process: he or she may fear being 'put on the spot' or being made to feel foolish. The coach can overcome this by spending time at the start of the relationship reassuring the coachee about how they are going to work together and what coaching actually involves.

Lack of confidence

Coachees who lack confidence may be reluctant to enter into a dialogue with their coach. Many coaching situations will involve looking at the coachee's confidence level, not just about interacting with the coach but about the skill or job being discussed. A major part of the coach's role is to help learners by enabling them to see the positives in their performance and thus build up their self-confidence.

Lack of motivation

Motivation is an internally generated attitude and every individual comes to any learning experience with different levels of motivation. Some may have been forced to attend against their wishes. Others may not see the reason for the coaching. Yet others may feel that they already know what they think the coaching is going to cover. One fact is certain – you cannot motivate people to learn. What you can do is provide all the factors available to encourage them to motivate themselves.

Fear of change

Change is frequently an unwanted event, usually because it is feared. The principal purpose of coaching is to produce change, whether this is a change in processes, knowledge, skill, attitudes or behaviour. Previous changes may have resulted in unwanted results. The coach needs to consider how the coachee is responding to change, and encourage commitment to change by clearly communicating the benefits/results intended from the experience.

Fear of failure

If the fear of change is not a barrier to motivation, the fear of failure may be. Fear of failure may be the result of previous failures. The coach obviously cannot ensure success, but if the coaching process is implemented effectively, there should be a minimized chance of failure.

'Old dog' syndrome

The belief that 'you can't teach old dogs new tricks' is in fact not completely true. If an older person has kept his or her mind active and in a learning mode, that person's experience may well mean he or she is in a better position to learn than a younger person. While this syndrome often emerges when older workers attend learning events during the last few years of their careers, the 'old dog' excuse is used for a variety of other barriers, including 'Why bother at this stage in my life?' To overcome this, you need to explore the individual's true reasons for not wanting to make the changes, as well as the benefits if he or she does. Having examples or role models that the person can identify with will help.

Physical/mental condition

If learners are experiencing physical discomfort (eg they are too hot, or hungry, or in pain) this can affect their ability to concentrate and learn. The coach should endeavour to ensure adequate refreshment, breaks and the right environment to limit the effect of physical discomfort. If the coachee is mentally pre-occupied this will also affect his or her ability to learn.

Personal working styles

When working with others it is useful to know that there are five distinctly different working styles, also known as 'drivers'. Drivers occur outside our awareness – they are subconscious attempts by us to behave in ways which will gain recognition from others. There are five drivers, as described by Julie Hay in her book *Working it Out at Work: understanding attitudes and building relationships*.

Hurry Ups

Hurry Ups work to get things done quickly and efficiently in the shortest possible time. Their major strength is the amount they can deliver; they respond well to deadlines and their energy peaks under pressure. Their underlying motivation is to do everything as soon as possible and they feel good if they complete tasks in the shortest possible time. They will say things like 'Quick', 'Get going', 'Hurry up', and 'Don't waste time'. They may speak quickly and will usually be doing more than one thing at a time. Non-verbal behaviour displayed by a Hurry Up includes foot tapping, finger tapping and checking of the watch. Hurry Ups' distress is caused by having time to think, silence and having nothing to do.

When coaching Hurry Ups be aware that they might become frustrated at the planning and reflection stages of the process and that they may want to see immediate improvements in their performance. Whilst you can take this into account when you are planning the coaching programme, you cannot avoid these stages altogether and you may need to give additional support to the Hurry Up coachee to help him or her complete the process fully. Things that you could try which would support Hurry Ups include:

- Praising them for their efficiency.
- Enjoying their spontaneity.
- Not being intimidated by their energy, enthusiasm or outbursts, but acknowledging these features and talking about why they are happening.
- Not advocating speed or the benefits of being able to do several things at once.
- Encouraging them to take time and thanking them for the time that they are committing to the coaching process.

Try Hards

Try Hards display determination and enthusiasm in their work. Their working style is all about putting effort into a task. They are good at seeing the big picture and when involved in project work they will be recognized for the way in which they follow up all the possibilities in a very thorough way. However, they may lose interest before the end of a task or project as they are more committed to trying than succeeding. They will use words or phrases such as 'Try', 'This is a better approach or idea', 'Can you. . .'. They fire off lots of questions – sometimes the Try Hard person strings so many questions together that the listener may need to work out what question to respond to. When asked questions, Try Hards may well answer a different question and often their sentences go off on tangents. Non-verbal behaviour includes a puzzled or frowned expression, sitting forward, an impatient manner and clenched fists. Being criticized for not caring or for being irresponsible causes their distress; being told 'You're not trying' will be a big issue for them.

When coaching Try Hards help them to clarify their goals and direction and encourage them to focus on completion of activities. Never let them off what they have committed themselves to do and don't praise trying: praise finishing. If the coachee is being very competitive, ignore it. Do not get involved in arguments that focus on comparisons.

Be Strongs

Be Strong people stay calm under pressure; they are self-sufficient and task orientated. They feel energized when they are able to cope and will still think logically when others around them are panicking. Be Strongs are considered to be steady and reliable workers whose strong sense of duty and ability to detach from emotions will help them tackle the most unpleasant tasks. This type of coachee hates admitting weaknesses and will come to regard failure as a weakness. He or she will tend to become overloaded with work, rather than admit to not being able to cope. These people may be highly self-critical about their shortcomings as well as considering as weak those who do ask for help. Verbal behaviour includes 'The facts here are. . .', 'Let me sort it out' and 'I will work 15 hours tomorrow to complete it'. Be Strongs do not ask for help easily, therefore they may find the whole idea of coaching difficult. Non-verbal behaviour includes immobile face and body (because they are trying to hide any evidence of feelings that may mean weakness), dispassionate tone of voice, straightening of clothes and an aloof manner. Be Strongs will become distressed when they fear rejection because they may be seen as vulnerable, being forced to say what they feel and exposing their weaknesses.

Coaching a Be Strong may be highly challenging, especially if your work style is profoundly different. Here are some things that you can do when working with Be Strongs:

- Be factual rather than effusive and emotional.
- Praise them for consideration and kindness as they often get taken for granted.
- Encourage them to delegate and to take on realistic amounts of work.
- Do not force them into expressions of vulnerability, but encourage them to express their feelings more openly.
- Do not shout, or they will retreat even further.
- When action planning with Be Strongs, spell out exactly what each task involves, so that they only do what is expected of them.

Be Perfect

The motto of the Be Perfect is 'If a job is worth doing, it is worth doing well'. This driver is the opposite of the Hurry Up. Be Perfect types strive for perfection and excellence, first time and with no errors. They check facts and detail, they plan ahead and are well organized. Sometimes their drive for perfection means that they miss deadlines as, for example, they need to check for mistakes and make minor alterations to layout. They have high expectations and fail to recognize when a lower standard would be appropriate and equally acceptable. They make statements like 'That's right', 'Perfect', 'Obviously', 'There's something missing here' and 'Actually. . .' . Non-verbal behaviour includes pursing of lips, smart and coordinated dress, controlled tone and obsessive/compulsive habits. Their distress is caused by anything that indicates the danger of loss of control, eg others' perceived low standards or illogical behaviour, over-emotionalism from other people and failure to achieve goals.

When coaching Be Perfects it is important to be punctual and keep the agreements that you have with them. Set pragmatic, rather than perfect, performance standards and always work with facts rather than emotions. If you do have to confront them, do it gently and firmly and if you have a difference of opinion, express your own thoughts with conviction. Explore with them the consequences of less than perfection and explain that it is OK to make mistakes.

Please People

These are good team members, who enjoy being with other people; their aim is to please others without asking, to work out what others would like and then provide it. They are understanding and empathetic and strive for harmony. They spend a lot of time smiling and nodding at people to indicate their agreement with them. When criticized by others they tend to take the criticism personally and may be upset. They let people interrupt them. They are hesitant to ask questions because they feel they should somehow know the answer. They say things like 'Really', 'I thought you might like to', 'Is that OK with you?' and are reluctant to say 'No'. Their non-verbal behaviour includes a lot of smiling, allowing others to interrupt them and good listening. Please People are distressed by being ignored and/or criticized. Please People coachees fear that they will be rejected by being found to be blameworthy.

If you have Please People coachees, encourage them to get in touch with their own needs and ask for what they want from the process. Be careful that they do not turn the coaching programme into an exercise of keeping you happy. You need to keep the focus all the time on them and be careful not to express your own wants. When you are giving feedback, it needs to be couched very positively in order to ensure that the coachees will be able to take the content 'on board', rather than using it to 'beat themselves up'.

When not under stress, drivers will appear as strengths and the beneficial side of them will become more obvious. Individuals who are not under stress do not have strong needs to gain recognition from others. When stress levels are high, the disadvantages of the drivers are more apparent as individuals seek to become more of what they think they should be – ie the driver takes over. The role of the coach is to create an environment that helps reduce stress and encourages coachees to accentuate the positives of their drivers.

Areas and levels of learning (Bloom's taxonomy)

Learning can be separated into three distinct areas (domains) which are categorized into different levels. Each level deals with a progressively higher and more complex type of learning. The three areas are:

Cognitive domain (knowledge)

This is related to the acquisition and application of knowledge and understanding. It deals mainly with learning of an intellectual nature. The levels within it are:

- Knowledge. This is the recalling or recognition of information as it was learnt, ie remembering.
- Comprehension. This is where the individual demonstrates understanding of the material and is able to interpret, not just recall, the information, ie understanding.
- Application. At this level the individual is able to use the information to solve problems.
- Analysis. This is where the information can be broken down into parts, and examined in order to make inferences from it.
- Synthesis. This is using knowledge that has been acquired in an original way, by applying the information to a new situation creatively.
- Evaluation. This is the highest level of learning, where an individual is able to judge the merits of an idea, make value judgements and offer his or her own views.

Affective domain (attitudes)

This domain is concerned with attitudes and feelings which are brought about or altered as a result of some learning experience. It deals with learning which has a substantial emotional basis. Learning in this domain is usually linked to learning in the cognitive domain. The levels within it are:

- Receiving. This is basically having an awareness of an idea and being willing to give attention to it.
- Responding. At this level, individuals display a positive interest in a topic or idea and react to it.
- Valuing. This is where individuals show some commitment to an idea.
- Organization. This is where individuals begin to develop an internally consistent value system, as they come to terms with an idea and modify their behaviour and views.
- Characterization. At this level individuals integrate the idea or concept into their life style by developing an attitude and behaviour consistent with it.

Psychomotor domain (skill)

This domain deals with the development of skills, largely of a physical nature. The levels within this domain are:

- Competency. The individual demonstrates the ability to carry out a skill, ie ability.
- Proficiency. The individual is able to perform a skill accurately, smoothly and with minimal effort, ie efficiency.
- Mastery. The person is able to perform the skill at the highest level and is able to adapt and originate. This is the expert level, where the individual is able to use the skill in new situations and creates new methods of operation.

3

Introducing the
coaching model

Whilst the key to successful coaching is about the relationship between the two people involved, it is possible to identify a process that can be followed to achieve the required outcome.

For a person who coaches on a regular basis, the process of coaching is a very integrated one but, like driving or even walking, there are various steps within the process that can be identified, even though in reality they may not appear to be separate at all. We have broken the coaching process down into these steps with the aim of helping you to think about what you need to do as a coach. As you become more experienced with this form of development you will reach the stage of unconscious competence and developing a coaching programme for your coachee will be as natural as walking or making a cup of tea.

There are three ways in which coaching might be initiated:

- An individual may have approached you directly and asked you to coach him or her, either because you are this person's line manager or because the individual thinks that you have skills/knowledge that would help.
- You have noticed that someone is not performing to his or her full capacity and feel that you could help this person by offering coaching.
- A third party, such as a person's line manager or a training department, may have asked you to coach the individual.

Whoever has initiated the coaching, however, we believe that there are six broad stages that need to be followed in any successful coaching relationship:

DO SOMETHING
Stage 1
Clarifying the overall need for, and
goals of, the coaching programme
Stage 4
Doing a task or activity from
the plan

THINK ABOUT IT
Stage 1
Clarifying the overall need for, and
goals of, the coaching programme
Stage 5
Reviewing activities and
planning for improved
performance

*The coaching process includes
all elements of the learning
cycle*

DO IT DIFFERENTLY
Stage 3
Formulating a detailed
plan
Stage 6
End the coaching relationship

MAKE SENSE OF IT
Stage 2
Agreeing specific development
needs
Stage 5
Reviewing activities and
planning for improved
performance

Figure 3.1 The coaching process mapped onto Kolb's learning cycle

1. Clarifying the overall need for, and goals of, the coaching programme.
2. Agreeing specific development needs.
3. Formulating a detailed plan for the coaching programme.
4. Doing a task or activity from the plan.
5. Reviewing activities and planning for improved performance.
6. Ending the coaching relationship.

The process may be followed from stages 1–6; however, in many instances you will find that in order to achieve your goals, you need to repeat stages 3–5 a number of times. This relates to the aim of coaching which is to achieve a persistent change in behaviour – to do this requires practice. Therefore coachees may require a number of experiences (practice sessions or doing it for real) and review discussions so that they can achieve their goals.

This systematic process of coaching links directly to Kolb's cycle of learning, as shown in Figure 3.1.

Our process model offers both a systematic and flexible approach, which can be adapted to suit both the environment and the individuals involved in the coaching relationship. Some steps may be quite short, or even merge into each other. At other times, you will be able to see each step quite separately. However, completely missing out stages in the process will have a profound impact upon the learning experience of coachees, as they will not have experienced the whole learning cycle required to formulate a persistent change of behaviour. Chapters 6 to 11 cover each of these stages in detail.

4

Job description, skills and qualities of a coach

You may be asking yourself how you fit into the model of coaching we have outlined. What will it involve? What is your role in the process?

Here is a generic job description for a coach:

Job description: Coach

Purpose: To work with individuals to improve their performance in a specific area or skill.

Key tasks and responsibilities

- Identifies development needs.
- Explains the coaching process to coachees, line managers and other stake-holders.
- Assists with the setting of learning goals and action planning.
- Uses a range of learning experiences to improve performance.
- Provides feedback for the coachee, based upon observed behaviour.
- Challenges the coachee's perception of his or her abilities.
- Helps the coachee to identify problems and possible routes to a solution.
- Supports the evaluation process by encouraging the coachee to assess progress against his or her learning goals.
- Helps the coachee to motivate self to achieve his or her learning goals.

Required skills/abilities

- planning and time management;
- analytical interpretation;
- negotiation;
- interpersonal skills;
  - building rapport
  - giving feedback
  - active listening
  - asking questions/gaining information
- observation;
- facilitation;
  - standard and goal setting
  - helping others learn
  - evaluation and review

Required qualities/attitudes

- supportive, empathetic;
- patient;
- positive attitude;
- respectful;
- trustworthy;
- honest;
- belief in people's potential;
- confident;
- objective and non-judgmental;
- sensitive;
- interested;
- perceptive;
- self-aware;
- attentive;
- retentive.

Required knowledge

Coaches require some knowledge of the subject that they will be coaching and specifically need to understand the expectations of performance; they do not need to be subject and/or technical experts. They also need knowledge of how adults learn and the theories of learning, along with the process of coaching.

5

Preparing to coach

Preparation for coaching will begin before you even have the initial conversation with your coachee to analyse the needs. In preparing to coach, we would suggest that you think about the following points.

Preparing yourself

- Consider who initiated the coaching process – do you need to consider how to work with third parties?
- Remind yourself of the role and responsibilities of a coach, perhaps by reviewing the coach job description and/or reviewing any documented corporate scheme.
- Get yourself into 'coach mode' – it is especially important to get yourself into the right frame of mind to coach if you are the coachee's line manager or have responsibilities for training – it is about 'putting on the right hat'.
- Put to one side any issues that might get in the way of you coaching someone else, eg your own work frustrations and 'to do' list – this is about clearing your mind so that you can focus all your attention on the coachee.
- Gather any equipment and/or information that you have or might need, eg brief from the coachee's line manager, coachee job description, company standards and targets, pens and papers.
- Refresh yourself about the coaching process to make sure you are clear about the steps that you will be taking, eg think about some questions that you will ask your coachee, read through the coaching model.

Preparing the coaching environment

- Book a quiet, private and comfortable space for your meetings (think about what the coachee will feel comfortable with, as well as what you will).
- Allocate sufficient time for the meetings.
- Order refreshments etc.

Preparing the coachee

- Communicate with the coachee the purpose of your first meeting – this will be best done verbally rather than via e-mail or memo; it initiates the rapport-building and will allow the coachee to ask any questions that he or she may have as well as giving you the opportunity to allay any fears.
- Tell the coachee where the meeting will be in good time for him or her to get directions or raise concerns.
- If you feel it is appropriate, you may want the coachee to begin to think about what he or she wants from the coaching process by asking some questions or giving the coachee a questionnaire to complete.
- Remind the coachee to bring any documents that might be relevant.

6

Stage 1: Clarifying
coaching needs and goals

By the end of this stage of the coaching process, you should have the following outcomes:

- Agreement that a development need exists and a broad idea of what that need is.
- An understanding, by the coachee and all stakeholders, of what coaching is and what the process will involve.
- Clearly stated goals for the coaching programme.

This is the first stage of the coaching process. During this stage the coach and the coachee will establish that there is a real need for coaching and will discuss the overall goals for the process. The specific objectives will come a little later – perhaps during the same meeting, or, more likely, during the next meeting.

What you do

The first thing you do is explore the reasons behind the request for coaching.
If *you* have initiated the coaching, ask yourself the following list of questions and be prepared to discuss your thoughts with the potential coachee.

- What makes you think that this person will benefit from coaching?
- What specific behaviours have you noticed that you would like to see changing?
- What do you want this person to be able to do better?

- What is the person not doing that you believe he or she is capable of?
- What achievements do you see this person being able to make as a result of coaching?
- What specific incidents can you describe that have led to you suggesting coaching?
- What have you told this person about why you think coaching would help him or her?
- Why have you chosen coaching, rather than other methods of development?
- What support will you be able to give this person during the coaching period and beyond?
- What do you think the impact of any changes in this person will be on the team and on others with whom the person comes into contact? What might the coachee need to do to deal with this impact?

If the *coachee* has initiated the coaching, it may be worth sending the person a revised version of this list of questions so that he or she can put some thought into his or her reasons for wanting coaching before your first meeting. This list of questions may then become the agenda for the first part of your initial meeting.

Is coaching the right approach?

In order to make sure that coaching is appropriate, very simply, go back to the definition of coaching:

> *The process of helping people **enhance** or **improve** their performance through reflection on how they apply a specific skill and/or knowledge.*

Once a development need has been identified the main question is how will this need be fulfilled – is coaching the appropriate answer?

The key questions to ask yourself at this stage are:

- Does the person already have the skill or knowledge to perform this task?
- Will the person be performing the task in the near future?
- If you work with this person on a one-to-one basis, will you be able to help the person enhance or improve the relevant aspect of his or her performance?

If the answer to these questions is 'Yes', then coaching is probably the way forward. If the answer is 'No' then the following learning methods should be considered:

- classroom training;
- e-learning;
- on-the-job training;
- self-study material;
- action learning.

Other factors that need to be considered before starting the coaching process are:

- Does the potential coach have the skill or knowledge that this person is going to use?
- Do the potential coach and coachee have the time to participate in the coaching process? Have you considered the implications on productivity?
- Does the potential coach have well-developed coaching skills?
- Are there any known relationship issues between the potential coach and the coachee, eg previous conflicts?
- Does the coach have a clear understanding of what the development goal is and how to measure its achievement?
- Are there standards/competency statements laid down against which performance will be assessed?
- Is the coachee aware that he or she has the development need?
- Is the coachee willing to be coached?
- Is the chosen coach willing to coach this coachee?
- Has the coach considered the implications of coaching this person for the rest of his or her team members?

Initial conversations

Having explored the needs for coaching individually you now enter the most crucial part of this stage, which is discussing these with the coachee. While this could happen over the telephone, there is much to gain by having a face-to-face meeting. The aim is to have an honest and open conversation around the question 'Why are we here?'. This is also an opportunity to explore what you both understand about the purpose of coaching in general, ie that coaching is not necessarily remedial and is actually about moving performance forward from where it is today, whether this performance is good or poor.

Another point to make during this conversation is your motive as the coach. This is especially important if you have an existing relationship with the person as he or she may be wondering about this. If you are the person's line manager you may be viewed with extreme suspicion unless you explain exactly what you are doing and why you are doing it. Equally, if you are not the coachee's line manager, he or she may wonder why you are doing this, what it really means, who else knows and what you will be getting out of it.

Part of this conversation will be about explaining the model of coaching so that the coachee understands the systematic approach that you are intending to follow. Go through the model and, if appropriate, give the coachee a copy of the process (shown in Chapter 3). As well as being open about the process, this allows the opportunity for you to tailor it to specific styles of working and opens the discussion about other requirements such as working hours and meeting places. This is also where you can talk about how you are going to work together, including any feedback that you will be giving to the coachees' managers, or others; requirements that you both should meet such as being on time for meetings or the coachee completing 'homework'. Explain to the coachee your ethics and stance on confidentiality, making mistakes and receiving feedback yourself. Ask the coachee if there are any ground rules that he or she would like you both to work with.

At the end of your meeting, ask the coachee if he or she feels that you will be able to work together. Chances are that the person will not say 'No', but the way in which 'Yes' is said will tell you a great deal. Observe body language, listen to the tone of voice used and decide whether you need to probe any further.

You may not wish to continue coaching this person if:

- You cannot get on. There is little rapport between you and you question whether you will be able to work together in this way. Rapport takes some time to build, but you will have an initial feel for how your relationship is likely to develop. Remember that you do not have to like each other, but you do need to have mutual respect and be able to establish a working relationship. If you feel that rapport can never be developed, now is the time to withdraw from the relationship.
- You don't feel that you are the right person to coach because you feel that you do not have enough knowledge of the subject matter. Depending on what you are coaching, it is not essential that you are able to perform at the level that the coachee is attempting to achieve. You need enough experience and knowledge of the subject matter to be able to help identify where the coachee could do better and help steer him or her towards the identified targets or standards.
- Having talked to the coachee you don't feel that coaching is the right development solution. It may become apparent that the coachee has training needs or even that his or her learning or communication style is such that the intense nature of the coaching relationship will not be right for this person.

Having established the overall development needs and decided that coaching is the right solution, you need to summarize the main points and create clear goals for the coaching that are agreed with your coachee. A development goal describes the overall purpose of what you will be doing. It describes what the coachee hopes to achieve from the process – the goal is about deciding where you are going, not how you will get there.

If practical, record this conversation in writing, and pass a copy of your notes to the coachee, so that you have the same understanding of what went on and an agreed way forward. Your notes here can then feed into Stage 2 of the process where you set the specific objectives for the coaching (see Chapter 7).

What could go wrong

The coachee didn't know that you had been asked to coach him or her and therefore wonders why you are arranging a meeting.

Discounting the option that the coachee is 'in denial', that is, he or she has been told, but tells you that this hasn't happened, the most usual situation is that he or she really has not been told. This might be for a variety of reasons:

- The person's manager has forgotten, being very busy with other things.
- Poor communication and the general personal relationship between the manager and member of staff means that the manager has not initiated the conversation, because he or she is unsure how to, or prefers not to.
- The manager wants to abdicate all responsibility to you, usually because he or she fears the reaction of the staff member and/or this is the easy option.

The solution is the same for any of the reasons listed and is formed from the desire to maintain the relationship with the coachee. Talk about what coaching is, how you got involved, the potential benefits for the coachee and what the process will involve – then ask the coachee if he or she is happy to proceed. If the coachee is happy to go on, then you can continue with the meeting.

If the coachee is not happy, it is not possible to proceed. You can ask some questions such as, 'What could we do to make you more comfortable with this?' or 'Why do you think your manager suggested this?' Fundamentally, however, coaching is a two-way relationship and if one party does not wish to participate you cannot be successful. Together you will need to agree how this decision is communicated to the line manager; either the coachee talks to the manager, you talk to the manager or you talk to him or her together. Wherever possible it is good to encourage the coachee to take responsibility and own his or her own decisions; therefore the ideal is to get the coachee to talk to his or her line manager. Follow up with both parties afterwards to review the situation and check that both parties are still happy.

The coachee doesn't agree to your ground rules.

The whole point of ground rules is to get agreement about how you will work together. You need to use your negotiation and influencing skills to arrive at an agreed position. Probe to establish the underlying reasons why some ground rules are acceptable and others are not – often this is about perception and understanding of the language that is being used. Remember that your disagreement may arise from some of your own personal beliefs, so ask yourself 'Is it really that important on this occasion and, if so, why?'

Your existing relationship may get in the way.

Given that you may be the coachee's line manager, are you the right person for the coachee to share his or her fears and doubts with? Can you maintain the role of coach no matter what the coachee tells you? Line managers can be very effective coaches by being clear about the purpose of their actions and explaining this to the member of staff. What gets in the way, if you are the person's line manager as well as the coach, is the coachee's concern that you are criticizing or telling him or her off. As coach, you need to be very honest at the start of each meeting about what the purpose of the discussion is and what role you are taking. Therefore, we recommend that if you are offering coaching to overcome a poor performance situation, you separate the giving of feedback from the start of the coaching process. Another solution here may be to find another coach from within or outside the organization.

The coachee doesn't want to be coached or sees it as a bad reflection on his or her abilities.

Your role here is to 'sell' the concept of coaching and to explain the developmental nature of the process. It is useful here to be able to explain the concept of continuous development – that however good we are already, we should always strive for future development. Perhaps give examples of when you have coached or been coached in the past and how it has helped.

Skills required

- communication;
  - questioning

- – listening
- – interpreting non-verbal communication
- – summarizing
- – assertiveness
- interpreting and analysing information.

7

Stage 2: Agreeing specific development needs

By the end of this stage of the coaching process, you should have the following outcomes:

- A closer working relationship with the coachee (or a decision that you can not continue the coaching programme).
- Detail about the precise development needs.
- A clear picture of the coachee's current ability and background experiences, including training to date.
- Agreed objectives for the coaching programme, including success criteria.

The purpose of this stage is to effectively discover what the current position of your coachee is and where he or she wants or needs to get to; this will take place through building rapport and discussion with your coachee. This stage will involve a meeting with your coachee – this may be a continuation of the meeting at Stage 1 (see Chapter 6) or it may be a separate event.

What you do

Build rapport

In order to identify the development needs effectively you need to build rapport with your coachee. Rapport is having a relationship where you are comfortable with each other, there is no competition and the flow of conversation is very natural. Each person feels that they are being listened to and often, if you watch people who have rapport, you will notice that they have similar body language, tones and breathing patterns – they are 'in tune'.

Rapport building means establishing common ground and showing each other mutual respect. It is about establishing a relationship based on trust and honesty. It is important to begin the rapport building at this stage because at this point you are laying the foundations for the whole coaching experience. Rapport building involves good communication skills and showing the other person that you understand his or her view of the world – empathy. This in turn involves having a genuine interest in the other person.

Small talk is useful in helping build rapport; you might want to start by talking about the sort of day you have had, your journeys, shared or similar experiences, the latest news etc.

In order to establish credibility as a coach and build the trust of your coachee, you probably need to share some information about yourself, if you haven't already done so. At some point consider sharing information about your background and experience, explain your working style and perhaps why you have been selected to coach. Be wary, however, of coming over as patronizing or as a 'know it all' – nothing can kill rapport more quickly! In addition to telling coachees what you think they want to know, or what you want them to know, ask them what they would like to know about you. Some coachees may like to know this first, others will be happy to leave it until you have talked about their needs.

To get onto the other person's wavelength, watch and listen – what is the non-verbal communication telling you? We all give away clues to our preferences by the words we use: if someone you are talking to is using visual language, use the same sort of words and note that he or she will like to *see* things on paper or in reality. By matching and mirroring other people's behaviour (not mimicking) you can help make them feel more at ease and comfortable with you, and you will notice that in return they will become more responsive and receptive with you. (See Chapter 13 for more about using language and non-verbal communication).

As a coach, you are responsible for helping the coachee become comfortable – with you and with the process. This involves thinking about the environment as well as what you say and do. Meeting somewhere that the person will feel at ease, having drinks available, and good seating all helps.

Identify needs

Identifying needs requires two things to be established: first, what the current position is; second, what the desired end position looks like.

Let's look at the first one – what is the current position? This is about clarifying where individuals are – what skills and knowledge they have and how they would rate their existing ability in the specific area. It is important here to use self-appraisal and open questioning as much as possible.

Discuss with the coachee what has brought him or her to this point – what training and what experience has he or she had? As the coachee answers these points, encourage him or her to give examples and evidence to back up his or her views, especially if the coachee has had feedback from others.

A good technique is to ask a coachee how he or she feels when doing the task; as a general guide, we usually feel good about the things we are better at, and vice versa. Negative feelings can arise from some doubt in our heads about our capabilities or uncertainty about what others think.

Try to get the person to think wider than the immediate task or process; and to relate any similar activities that he or she has experienced which may be relevant. Considering other tasks that use a similar set of skills can also help coachees identify the areas that they want to look at.

Some questions for clarifying needs are:

- How did you learn what you know about this subject/activity?
- What training have you had on this subject/activity?
- What experience did you have before your training?
- What experience have you had since your training?
- How do you feel about this subject/activity?
- What feedback have you had about your performance around this subject/ activity?
- What examples can I see of your performance in this subject/activity?
- What skills do you use when you are performing this activity?
- In what other situations do you use these skills?
- Is there any specific part of this task that you find easy or enjoy doing? Why?
- Is there any specific part of this activity that you find difficult or do not like?
- Why do you think you find this aspect of the task problematic?
- What factors do you think influence how you perform this task?

Next it is vital to describe the desired outcome. This is the second part of identifying needs – assessing current competency depends on having a clear benchmark against which to assess.

Rather than assume or work towards an invisible goal, an essential part of coaching is asking coachees what they want to achieve and how they will know when they have been successful. Some will have a clear goal in mind: 'I want to be able to do. . .', others will initially just want to get better or feel more confident. These latter statements need to be explored and made more visual. Asking the following questions will help:

- What would you like to be able to do by the end of this coaching experience?
- What does 'better' look like?
- If others were to give you feedback in two months' time, what would you like them to say?
- How will you know when you have improved?
- Do you know anyone else who is better than you at this? What do they do?
- When do you think you can apply this skill? What do the good performers do that you would like to be able to do?

In identifying the desired outcome it may be useful to refer to corporate or nationally recognized standards or competency frameworks.

While you are having this discussion, you may want to make some notes. We all have different ways of recalling conversations. Some of us are able to rely on our memory; others (including us!) need to jot notes down. These are not formal, but are aide memoires. If you decide to make notes, explain to your coachee what you are writing and the reasons for writing it as people worry about what might happen to the notes. Another option is to ask the coachee to write the notes – although be careful that this does not distract the coachee away from thinking about the questions that you are asking.

Develop the objectives

This is the stage of the process where you agree what the coaching process is going to achieve – what are the outcomes and targets you will work towards together. This can take place during the meeting or you can go away with your notes and produce a list of what you perceive the objectives to be and send them to the coachee for comments – they can then be discussed, either at another meeting or over the telephone. If you choose to correspond about the objectives via e-mail, follow up the final version with a phone call or meeting to check how the coachee really feels about things.

The broad goal(s) that you agreed during Stage 1 (see Chapter 6) now needs to be broken down into more detailed objectives, which reflect the needs you have analysed. Coaching objectives turn the goal into measurable outputs. An objective is a specific statement of something the coachee will be able to do at the end of the coaching process.

Before agreeing the objectives with the coachee, in addition to remembering the needs that you have already identified, it will be worth revisiting the following questions:

- What is any third party (eg line manager, HR department) expecting to see at the end of the coaching process ?
- How much time has been allocated for the coaching?
- What factors are likely to impact upon the coaching, eg changes of work deadlines for the coachee, available resources, working hours?

Effective objectives

When creating objectives, focus on the coachee – what will this person be able to do as a result of being coached? It is vital to remember that the coaching process is not about the coach and what he or she wants to achieve. The process is about what the coachee needs and wants to achieve and therefore all the objectives that are written must be about the needs of the coachee.

A good opening statement for objectives is: 'Having completed this coaching programme you will be able to. . .'. Starting each objective with this statement will focus it on the specific behaviour that the coachee will demonstrate as a result of the coaching and will cause the coach to concentrate on 'SMART' objectives.

SMART objectives

SMART has become a well-known acronym to describe well-constructed objectives. SMART objectives have the following characteristics:

- They are **specific** – they focus on a particular aspect of the individual's performance or on the job/task in question.
- They are **measurable** in that their achievement can be assessed and there will be a visible outcome when they are achieved.
- They are **agreed**. This is particularly pertinent to the coaching situation where it is absolutely vital that the coach, coachee and, where applicable the third party, have all agreed on the objectives for the coaching programme.
- They are **realistic**. Again this is vital in the coaching process. If the objectives are not realistic then the coaching will fail. This may result in demotivation of both coach and coachee and in the line manager losing faith in the coaching process.
- They are **timed** in that there is a time frame set for their achievement. From the perspective of the coach, coachee, manager and organization, setting

time frames for the coaching programme is very important so that all concerned will know what to expect in terms of how long the process will take and what can be achieved in the time allocated.

Another acronym which is often applied to objectives is SMAC: specific, measurable, achievable and challenging.

Take time to think about the words that you use when you create your objectives. These words will inform your choice of method and provide a guide for measuring the achievement of the objectives. Non-measurable words include 'understand', 'value', 'appreciate', 'enjoy', 'feel', 'believe' and 'know'.

Good words for objectives are:

Describe	Explain
List	Write
Demonstrate	Operate
Perform	Complete
Deal with	Run
Facilitate	Achieve
Create	Produce
Process	Communicate
Make	Check
Train	

Having finalized the objectives the coach should put them in writing so that the coachee and any other individuals who have a stake in the coaching programme can review them. This way there can be no misunderstandings about what the programme is and is not setting out to achieve.

At this point the coach and coachee need to agree that achievement of the objectives will meet the identified needs. Are all the needs reflected in the objectives or has anything been missed or misinterpreted? Of course, as the coaching programme proceeds objectives may change. If this happens then the new objectives should also be put in writing and circulated to all those involved. It may be useful for the coach, coachee and line manager to sign the objectives document to confirm that all are in agreement about the objectives for the programme.

What could go wrong

You don't feel that you are the right person to coach.

You feel that you do not have enough knowledge of the subject matter.

Depending on what you are coaching, it is not essential that you are able to perform at the level that the coachee is attempting to achieve. You need enough experience and knowledge of the subject matter to be able to help identify where the coachee could do better. A more valuable asset is the ability to facilitate the coachee's learning and to explore options for improvement. Bearing this in mind, if you still don't believe that you are the right person, after tactfully explaining why to the coachee, help him or her to find someone else.

Time frames are too short.

Having got a better feel for the development needs you are aware that the time frames that you have been given are too short or other things will take priority. At this point you will need to renegotiate the time frames or do whatever is necessary for you both to free up the time for coaching. Alternatively, consider reducing the number of objectives.

It is a training issue not a coaching issue.

Let's go back to our definition of the difference between these two activities – it is a training issue if there is a gap in the skills and or knowledge required to carry out the task; it is a coaching issue if the skills or knowledge exist, but the individual cannot implement them fully to achieve the required level of performance. In this case you can either stop coaching and begin training or have the training need met from a third party (training course, distance learning etc). If you choose to train, be clear both for yourself and the coachee which hat you are wearing and when, to avoid any confusion about method and approach.

You have not allowed enough time to complete this meeting.

You may find that your discussion with the coachee about his or her needs and the subsequent objective setting is going to take longer than you thought. The best thing to do in this situation is to end the meeting once you have analysed the needs and to set another time where you will discuss objectives. As soon as you are aware that time is running out, you should start to renegotiate how you will complete this stage.

You are unable to get to the bottom of the needs.

You find that you are unable to really identify the difference between the current and the desired position. Your questions do not provide you with the information that would enable you to see what needs to be changed in order for the coachee to perform better. In this case perhaps the coachee could return to his or her workplace and get feedback from colleagues and line manager. Alternatively you could volunteer to observe the coachee and give some feedback yourself. The real need might be around self-confidence – the coachee may be performing to a high standard, but be self-critical or unsure. It might even be that there is no development need and that this conversation has been enough in itself to bolster the coachee's confidence.

Skills required

The following skills are required at Stage 2 of the coaching process:

- analytical skills;
- verbal and written communication skills;
  - negotiation skills
  - questioning
  - listening
  - presenting information
  - rapport building
- summarizing;
- time management;
- facilitation.

8

Stage 3: Formulating a detailed plan for coaching

By the end of this stage of the coaching process, you should have the following outcomes:

- A detailed plan for the coaching programme.
- Clear steps for achieving the development objectives.
- A timescale for the coaching programme.

Having agreed the objectives for the coaching, the next thing that needs to be considered is how the objectives will be achieved. This stage is about formulating a plan which details how you will proceed during the coaching process.

What you do

You must formulate the plan with your coachee, not present it as a *fait accompli*. If others are involved in the plan, communicate the relevant parts of the plan to them as well.

The general plan for the coaching will include and take into account:

- A review of each of the objectives. This means looking at each objective and asking:
  - What does this objective mean?
  - What activities need to take place in order to achieve this objective?
  - Will the activities be real or simulated?

- When do the activities need to happen? This will be particularly important where the objectives relate to specific tasks that the coachee does at certain times in the week, month or year.
- The time available for coaching.
  - Time for each meeting.
  - Time for the whole process.
- Preliminary tasks that the coachee will need to carry out – such as refresher reading or gathering data.
- Involvement of others. The topics of the coaching may involve other people, eg the coachee may wish to improve his or her skills in leading meetings.
- Equipment required.

As the coaching process is linked very closely to Kolb's learning cycle, as illustrated in Chapter 2, your plan must include each of the following at least once:

Having an experience

The coachee needs to have an experience, that is, to do the task or use the skill that the coaching is concerned with. This experience may be real or simulated. It may be planned or unplanned. It may be observed by the coach or described by the coachee. Whatever the subject, the coachee must carry out the task or do the activity in as near real-life situation as possible. The type of experiences that you may use during coaching are:

- Doing all or part of the task.
- Seeking and receiving feedback.
- Revisiting activities that have been done in the past.
- Completing self-assessment questionnaires.
- Reading books, articles or other documentation.
- Finding out how others do it.
- Observing others.

Reflecting on the experience

This is where the main activity of the coach begins and, as such, it needs to be shown as an action or activity on the plan. The role of the coach is to provide the coachee with tools to help him or her reflect upon the experience and start to draw out some learning from it. It will involve thinking and discussing the experience, what happened, the outcome(s) from it and how the people involved felt.

Making sense of the experience

In practice, this will happen as the coachee reflects on the experience. This is where the coach helps the coachee to think about why things happened the way they did. What were the underpinning processes? What was going on 'behind the scenes'?

Doing it differently

In coaching, this is where the coach and coachee discuss and identify what the coachee could do differently the next time and what he or she should repeat. This is the 'planning for next time' phase.

Repeating the experience

The coachee should then have the opportunity to do the task or activity again, incorporating the ideas that were discussed during the coaching session.

Your plan may then be to repeat the reflection–making sense–planning activities–repeating experience until the coaching objectives have been achieved.

Part 3 offers you a series of activities to use as part of the coaching process. These activities are for you to select from, deciding which will be appropriate for the subject of your coaching and your coachee.

What could go wrong

There is no opportunity for the coachee to practise in real life.

The first thing to question in this case is why coaching is taking place now. If coaching is about helping a person implement skills and knowledge back in the workplace, the ideal time for coaching is either immediately before that person is required to do a particular task or whilst he or she is doing it. Therefore, you may want to postpone the coaching until it is more relevant to the coachee's current work.

However, there may be situations where coaching needs to take place even if the task is not going to be performed for some time. An example of this would be where you have been asked to coach someone in crisis management. You will not want to wait until a crisis happens, and you will not be able to predict when this will be, so coaching needs to happen when the coachee and coach are available and will take place around a simulated event.

There are too many things to do, for either the coach or coachee.

This is likely to occur if the task is very large and/or you are working to very tight timescales. Remember to be realistic when you are planning. It is easier, and better for motivation, to move dates forward than to put them back or not achieve at all. 'Under-promise, over-achieve.'

Have a look at your plan and think about which of the activities could be taken out of it, eg, would it be possible to leave out the reading or to have someone else observe the coachee?

The coachee or coach may need to negotiate with his or her line manager to have some time freed up for the coaching process – whether this is possible will depend on the priority that is placed upon the coachee improving his or her performance in the area concerned.

Skills required

- planning;
- prioritizing.

9

Stage 4: Doing a task or activity

By the end of this stage of the coaching process, you should have the following outcomes:

- A completed task or activity.
- Evidence of how the coachee has performed on which to base your reflection/review.

The fourth stage of the coaching process is to start to implement your agreed plan. It is about focusing on carrying out your planned activities so that together, in the next stage, you can work on the specific areas/behaviours that will need to be changed in order for the overall performance to be improved.

Your plan will involve actions under two main categories: first, application – practising the job/task or activity that the coachee wants to improve; second, collecting data and evidence about how well the coachee has done during that practice. Evidence in this sense means information about how the person has performed – this may be data gained via self-appraisal, observation, feedback or tangible results such as reports, statistical data or products.

What you do

This stage is about organizing and structuring the hands-on experience so that the coachee gets the most from it. It is where the coachee uses skills or knowledge in the way that he or she would in real life. That might mean carrying out a specific task or job (or a part of it) or doing something where he or she can practise applying, or think about applying, some of the appropriate skills or knowledge. This is the experience stage of the learning cycle.

There are two options: either the coachee does it for real; or you arrange a simulation. Both options have advantages but we prefer, wherever possible, getting the coachee to do it in the 'live' environment, either with you observing or with him or her reporting back to you on the experience or activity (see below).

If the subject is about applying a skill, it is about having the opportunity to use that skill in a real life situation (or similar). It is about the coachee demonstrating the knowledge, skill or behaviour so that, working with his or her coach, that individual can reflect upon it and identify where he or she goes to next.

Before the experience or activity takes place, you and the coachee need to:

- Arrange for the experience or activity to happen if it is not a regular part of the coachee's role.
- Discuss how to ensure that performance is as natural as possible.
- Consider how the coachee wants to use the experience or activity, ie what he or she wants to learn from it.
- Decide what help and support the coachee wants to receive during the actual experience or activity, ie define the points at which he or she wants you to intervene, observe or take part.
- Identify potential risk areas, eg 'What happens if I get this wrong at this stage and if I do, what will be the consequences? What mistakes can I make without causing irreparable damage?'
- Establish the starting and ending points for the experience or activity. This is particularly relevant if the activity is part of the coachee's day-to-day role.
- Decide how and when you will review the experience or activity – this might be immediately after the activity or later, or perhaps both.

Simulation or real life?

The starting point is deciding whether it is appropriate for the coachee to practise in real life – ie do the activity. Usually the coachee will have already done it for real as this is how a coaching need is identified. At some stage before the coaching relationship ends the coachee should do the task or activity in real life, so that you can really assess whether the coachee has achieved his or her goal. However, early on in the coaching programme, you may want to consider practising via a simulated situation; some of the questions you may want to explore with the coachee as you decide are:

- Is the timing right – is an opportunity to do it going to occur naturally within the workplace within the time boundaries of the coaching plan?
- Is it safe – for the coachee and for others involved in the activity?
- What are the implications of getting it wrong, eg lost business or reputation of the coachee with colleagues?
- Is the coachee confident and experienced enough to 'perform' in real life?

Using real life

Any experience that takes place in real life offers a more effective learning opportunity than a simulation. Doing a task or performing in real life means that it is impossible to control the environment and situation and therefore provides an authentic experience. When using real life experiences, consider:

- Which part of the experience is important at this stage of the coaching programme – will you review the activity in totality or focus this time on parts of it?
- Will you observe or not?
- What will you do if the experience doesn't provide the evidence that you want it to?
- What is your agreed strategy for dealing with errors or unexpected scenarios during the event? If you are present, does the coachee want you to intervene or take over if they are getting it wrong?
- Will you explain to others involved that you are using this as a coaching opportunity?

Using simulation

A simulation is the creation of a true-to-life event within a controlled setting. Simulations are used when it is not possible to observe or arrange a real experience for your coachee at an appropriate time during the coaching process.

This technique is very useful where mistakes with the subject being coached have the potential to cause major damage, losses or a disaster; for example, counselling or resuscitation. They provide a protected environment in which coachees can act and discuss their actions without fear of the consequences. The lack of consequences should be considered when reviewing a simulation as this may have an impact upon the way in which the coachee and participants act and react. It may also limit understanding of real life, eg when practising resuscitation, if I do not fear that I may kill someone, I may not fully understand that this could happen in reality.

Each simulation is unique. It is impossible to give guidelines that apply to all situations; however, factors to consider when you are creating a simulation are:

- What equipment will you need?
- What people need to be involved?
- Where will you do the simulation?
- How will you set up the simulation (brief the participants)?
- What background information do you need?
- How much time do you have available for the simulation?
- How can you recreate the real-life situation? How can you avoid the 'It's only make believe' reaction?
- How many times will you need to rerun this simulation and, if several times, how many different versions do you need?
- What elements need to be contained within the simulation (what should the content be)?

Collecting evidence

While the focus at this stage of coaching must be on performing an activity, as true-to-life as possible, in order for the coaching process to be effective, the coach and coachee need to be collecting information for discussion once the activity or experience is completed.

It is important that data collection does not detract from the activity and the best way of doing this is to consider what data you need and how you will collect it. It all comes back to knowing the objectives for the coaching. If you know what standards the coachee is working towards, you can work out what evidence will tell you how well he or she is doing against these standards and this will tell you what data you need to collect. You can then work out how you can collect the data in as unobtrusive a way as possible. It is recommended that you look for more than one data source.

Observation

Observation, the act of watching the coachee perform a task or activity, can be done in three different ways:

- The coach observes.
- Someone other than the coach is given the role of observer.
- The coachee is video-taped (or audio-taped if appropriate).

In deciding whether observation is the best method to use to achieve the coaching objectives, consider:

- Appropriateness of observing. What is the confidentiality of what you are likely to be observing, eg is it appropriate that you sit in on something like a counselling session or a disciplinary interview? Think about whether your presence will impact the event in such a way that it means it is not a true experience. Whilst the coachee may be happy for you to observe, other people may not be. People certainly should not be presented with a *fait accompli*; their permission must be sought prior to or at the start of the event.
- Environment. Is there space and is it safe for you to observe? For example, if your coachee is driving a specialized machine or doing something in a confined space, observing him or her will be impractical. Have you got the right equipment to attend the place of work, eg high visibility clothing or safety equipment?
- Time. It might be that the task that you are observing takes several days, so you may agree that you do not watch all of it, only parts. There may be a finite amount of time that has been allocated for the coaching (eg if a coach is being paid for externally or the coach can only be taken out of the workplace for a specific time), so this time may be better spent on other activities such as reviewing performance from recalled events or task outputs.
- Your ability to stay quiet and observe! Are you likely to interfere or take over?

Very few of us can observe an event and keep everything that we have seen and heard in our heads. There is a need to make notes and to avoid subjectivity. When we observe something, our natural response is to interpret what we see and to describe what we perceive is happening. For example: we hear someone shouting and we describe them as being angry and aggressive. We are interpreting their behaviour based on 'If I was doing that, it would be because I was. . .' or 'In my experience, people do that when. . .' . However, in our example, this person could be shouting because the other person cannot hear or because he or she was excited!

We need to ensure that we are objective and that our observations are based on the facts of what we have seen or heard – ie, to continue our example, we could note that the volume of the person's voice went up.

Tips for effective observation

- Prior to the experience, discuss with the coachee what you will be looking for, including what he or she wants you to look for.
- Write these criteria down one side of a page – then you can note down what the coachee says or does against the relevant point.
- Think about the key things you might see during the observation. Write down:
  - What you would expect to see.
  - What you would expect to hear.
  - What behaviours you would expect the coachee to demonstrate.
  - What you hope not to see.
  - Tick each time you see or hear each thing happening.
- In identifying what is truly happening, use any or all of your five senses that are appropriate for the task – avoid interpretation or intuition at this stage. You need to note *what* has happened not *why* you think it happened; you will discuss the *why* with the coachee later.
- If you do see or hear something and you think you know the reason for it happening, you may want to make a note of your thoughts as a memory jog for yourself later. Be cautious that this doesn't colour your impression of what happens next or influences the rest of your observation because you are solely looking for confirmation of your assumptions. Equally, when you come to review the task later with the coachee, remember to get the coachee to tell you why he or she did something rather than assuming your interpretation of the coachee's behaviour is the right one.
- Whenever creating your own shorthand, write yourself a key so that when you review your notes later, you will understand what you wrote.
- Choose a writing tool that lets you write quickly and that will not smudge. Always have a spare pen or pencil to hand.
- Take a note of the time at the start of the activity and the times of 'events' during the activity. Note the time when the activity finishes. This is useful when you are discussing your notes with the coachee as you can explain how long it took him or her to do certain things, you can review the pattern of action, and you can minimize disputes of when things did or did not happen.
- If observing something that involves other people, have a column where you can note those people's reactions or responses to what your coachee said or did.
- Have plenty of paper to hand and use a clipboard if you do not have a table to rest on.
- Keep your notes out of view of other people in the room.

The impact of observation

As coaches, we should be aware that some people will perform better because we are observing them, while some people's performance will worsen. The impact of observing your coachee will probably lessen the more you do it and the more the relationship develops – as long as the relationship is developing positively of course! This is known as the Hawthorne Effect, which originated from a series of experiments carried out within a factory setting. The researchers found that the act of simply observing workers at work had an impact upon their performance. In some instances this impact was positive and in some it was negative.

Another point to consider is that some people will perform, in the sense that they will 'act' for you in the way which they think they should act, rather than the way which they would normally act. We also need to remember that our impact may be upon others involved in the 'activity' not just on the coachee.

You can minimize the impact that you might have by reminding the coachee that you are not observing him or her in order to criticize – observation is a tool for gathering information which you will both discuss later. Stress to the coachee that mistakes are OK, so long as they do not put anyone at risk (see later in this chapter for more discussion about risks and when to intervene).

You will also need to explain to other participants in the activity exactly what the purpose of your observing the event is, how you will be doing it and that you need them to behave as normally as possible. Finally make yourself as unobtrusive as possible – do your best to blend in with the background by positioning yourself as much out of view as possible, without compromising your view of the coachee or causing a distraction.

Intervention – when and how

People learn from their mistakes and therefore we should not try to shield them or prevent them from making mistakes. There is a difference between helping somebody and taking over – however frustrating it may be to see someone struggling, you should resist the temptation to leap in saying 'No, no, let me do it'.

You must agree with your coachee, during the planning stage, the boundaries for the activity and the times when you will intervene. The times when it is appropriate to intervene fall into three broad categories:

- The coachee is going to harm him- or herself (either physically or mentally).
- The coachee is going to harm another person (either physically or mentally).

- The coachee is going to compromise the business or organization in some way.

You may also agree with your coachee that you will intervene if you see him or her exhibiting a certain behaviour that he or she is trying to work on and wants to receive feedback about immediately. The following are useful statements to use when intervening:

- 'I need to stop you there. Before you move on we need to discuss what's happening.'
- 'Stop now.' (Use in dangerous situations only).
- 'Before you do that, tell me what you are hoping will happen as a result of doing it.'
- 'You asked me to tell you if I saw you. . .'
- 'What you have just done is an example of what we talked about when. . .'

You may ask someone else to do the observation. This is especially useful when you are an integral part of the process or activity, or when you are unable to attend at the time that the coachee will be doing the task. The same guidelines apply and you may want to run through these with the nominated person beforehand.

Using video and/or audio tapes is useful when you can not attend or it isn't appropriate because of the nature of the job for you to be there – eg, your presence would change the relationship between the coachee and others involved. All participants should agree to be filmed or taped, and they must be informed about what will happen with the tapes. Another advantage is that you can re-play all or some of the tape to examine specific behaviours. However, on the down side, not many of us like to be video-taped, and this may have an adverse impact on performance. Audio tapes have the obvious difficulty that you can not see what has happened, so we prefer only to use these when coaching on telephone techniques or other situations when non-verbal behaviour is not involved.

Getting feedback from others

Third-party feedback can be very useful for coachees – how have others reacted to their behaviour and what impact has it had? We feel it is important that third-party feedback is always given directly to the coachee by the person that observed him or her and not given to the coach to 'pass on'. Feedback needs to be detailed and owned by the person giving it. Feedback that is passed on by another person can often be watered down or misinterpreted and there is no room for the person receiving it to ask for clarification or further detail. You may need to help your coachee ask for feedback and/or help the third party think about how he or she will give it.

To help your coachee ask for feedback, the two of you could role-play the situation until the coachee feels able to ask the other person, or help the coachee construct a questionnaire, which they discuss with the giver of feedback.

To help the third party give feedback, discuss why it is beneficial for the coachee to receive it at this time (without breaking confidences), explore why the third party prefers not to if this is the case and offer him or her guidelines to follow. (See the model for giving feedback in Chapter 10).

Sometimes you may plan to ask others involved in the activity for feedback. There is an argument for telling the third party beforehand that you will be asking. This will prepare him or her for your questions. However, we can also see that this could have a detrimental effect on the activity, because the third party is so busy assessing the performance of the coachee that it affects his or her behaviour.

Output data

Output is something you can physically see as a result of a task being completed. Most processes or tasks will have some form of output whether it be a report, a letter or a physical object such as a cake or brick wall. Wherever appropriate, arrange to receive a copy or sample of the output and use it to review against performance standards.

What could go wrong

The planned activity does not happen.

This could be because someone else cancels it, the business no longer requires it or unforeseen circumstances come into play. If this happens, then you either need to rearrange or, if that is impractical, look towards running a simulation. You may also consider doing something different from the planned activity.

The activity does not turn out to involve the things that you thought it would.

Perhaps it takes an unexpected turn of events or it does not provide the opportunity to practise the skills you thought it would. This is a golden opportunity to work with your coachee and discuss why events did not happen as planned and what can be learnt when this occurs. It might be that, on reflection, you could have pre-empted this at the planning stages.

Everything happens as planned but the coachee performs so badly, or has such a bad experience, that his or her confidence is shattered.

In this situation, you can't start analysing immediately – the coachee will not be ready to do so and will not be able to be positive about the experience. It is time to 'hug' the person – be supportive and upbeat, with the aim of helping the coachee restore his or her self-esteem.

Tell the coachee to tell you when he or she is ready to discuss the activity. When the coachee does tell you, you may find that you don't need to spend a lot of time reflecting on the experience, but can focus on 'If you were to do that again, what would you do differently?'. This gets away from reliving a bad experience and on to positive action for the future. You can continue the coaching as planned, with a silent agreement not to discuss this situation until the coachee is ready, if at all. Individuals have their own ways of dealing with things and it is not for us to insist that this is through discussion or analysis.

Skills required

- observation;
- listening;
- presenting information.

10

Stage 5: Reviewing activities and planning improved performance

By the end of this stage of the coaching process you should have the following outcomes:

- A list of the coachee's strengths and areas for development.
- A plan for what the coachee will do differently next time he or she performs the task or activity.

This stage incorporates reflection/discussion with the coach about what happened and how to improve next time the task is carried out. This is the part of the process where the coach and coachee meet to discuss the experience that the coachee has had and how the coachee can build upon this experience in order to improve his or her performance.

Key information that will feed into this stage of the process is:

- The coachee's perception of what happened and how he or she performed.
- The coach's observations.
- Comments and observations from third parties, eg customers, line managers, colleagues – gathered by the coachee.
- Comparison of the output of the activity to the required standard.

What you do

This is the point where coachees may start to feel vulnerable. They may feel as if you will be judging them or getting them to confess their weaknesses. Therefore, overcome some of these anxieties by starting with a reminder of the purpose of your discussions.

Explain to coachees that this is an important part of the learning process, the purpose of which is to review their performance during the activity with a view to assessing how near they are to achieving their coaching goals. To this end it is important that the coachee is open, honest and willing to discuss what happened. It may be a useful time to remind coachees that you are there to help and not to criticize or judge.

The whole point is to review what happened, the outputs and feelings, and compare them with the required performance outcomes. So it is important to revisit the original purpose for the coaching and review against your objectives.

Tips to help your coachee relax

- Arrange to meet in a neutral place.
- Allow sufficient time for a prolonged discussion.
- Focus your attention fully on the coachee – leave all your day-to-day distractions at the door.
- Use open questions to encourage discussion.
- Remember the impact of your body language and tone of voice.
- Ensure that the environment is comfortable – consider heating, lighting, seating, availability of refreshments etc.

Your role as a coach is to help progress the review discussion to encourage the coachee to evaluate his or her own performance – using your skills and qualities of questioning, listening, challenging, encouraging, observing and giving feedback to support the process.

There are three phases to this discussion. They are:

- Discussing what happened during the experience. Considering the facts and the implications of what happened.
- Discussing why things happened the way they did. Coming up with a set of theories about the experience.
- Discussing what might be done differently, how this will benefit the situation and consider what needs to be repeated.

What comes first – self-evaluation or feedback?

Self-evaluation is the art of reflecting on your own performance in as objective a way as possible. It involves thinking about what went well, what difficulties you experienced and what you would do differently next time. Feedback involves a third party describing to you what he or she heard or saw, the impact of this and what he or she would like to see in future.

So, should you get the coachee to self-evaluate and then give feedback or do you give feedback and then get the coachee to self-evaluate? Most writing on this topic advocates using self-evaluation first. The logic seems to be that if the person does this, he or she will be more likely to hear the evaluation and take notice of it. It is considered more beneficial for individuals to identify their own mistakes than to have them pointed out. It is all about ownership – if I identify my mistakes, I will own them and it is more likely that I will correct them; if someone else points out my mistakes I am more likely to get defensive and cling on to the old way of doing things.

We do not dispute the value of self-evaluation; however, our culture has conditioned us to look outside ourselves to validate what we are doing. A 'Well done' from our teacher generally means a good deal more than the feeling of 'I have done that well'. Even in adult life we all have examples of when we have felt good about something and have been disappointed by someone else's reaction. On occasions we may even have had the opposite response – we think we have done a mediocre job and someone else tells us it was excellent! In reality most of us want to know what the other people think and until we do we may not be able to give an honest self-appraisal. It is hard to open up and be honest if you think the other person may disagree.

Our conclusions are that there seem to be two options. Firstly, give some overall feedback and then let the coachee self-evaluate, eg 'Generally I thought you did very well; you picked up on most of the things we planned. What are your thoughts?'. The second option is to ask the coachee how he or she wants to structure the conversation with a statement/question such as 'I want to hear from you how you think it went; I also have some views of my own. How would you like to do this?'.

Sometimes when you have a specific message to give, self-evaluation used first can muddy the issue or not give you the platform you hoped for. For example, if the performance was poor, and the coachee's self-appraisal is that it was excellent, you have set up a potential conflict situation, which might have been avoided if you had given your feedback at the start. A second example could be where the coach asks the coachee what he or she could have done differently, the coachee says x, which is not the answer that the coach wanted.

The coach then asks what else, which shows the coachee that the coach has something in mind but introduces a guessing game. The motive could be kindness or the coach's need to be clever.

Fundamentally, your approach depends on the people involved and the situation. What we recommend is that you seriously consider your approach and what is right for the coachee.

Giving feedback – the coach's observations

The word feedback is used to describe constructive comment about actions, situations or issues. This means it can provide praise, as well as point out areas for improvement. Whatever process you use to give feedback, your motive is to help the other person develop. Consider the feedback that you are going to give and ask yourself two questions: Why am I doing this? How will it help the other person?

The following is a list of factors to consider:

- Concentrate on the behaviour not the person.
- Direct the feedback towards behaviour that the person can do something about.
- Be specific.
- Use observations not inferences.
- Give feedback as soon as possible after an event.
- Be clear about your motives.
- Give positive as well as negative feedback where appropriate.
- Don't overload a person with feedback.

Before giving feedback, consider the likely reaction of the coachee. Put yourself in the coachee's shoes – what might he or she say? This will help you to plan and be prepared for whatever might happen.

Model for giving feedback

- Tell the person what you have observed. Concentrate on performance and behaviour (what we do) rather than personality (what we are). Give specific examples that the person can link to the precise behaviour and circumstances.
- Explain the result of what you have observed. For this, you need to ask yourself 'How did the behaviour affect the situation or people involved? What was the general effect and how did you think or feel?'. This could be a good or negative impact and you need to explain why it was good or bad.

- State that you want to look at options for the future. Initiate a conversation about options for improvement or change, or how to maintain good performance.

Receiving feedback

One of the challenges of giving feedback is our fear of how the other person will receive the message that we are giving. As a coach, you may need to help your coachee with some tips on how to receive feedback and you need to be prepared to receive feedback yourself. Coaching should be a two-way process; your coachee may want to comment on how you have performed or behaved during the process and we would encourage you to actively seek this evaluative information.

Some coaches may not ask for feedback because:

- They feel that the whole process should be focused on the coachee and therefore they have no right to ask for the feedback.
- They believes that they must 'play the teacher' and therefore it would not be appropriate to ask for feedback.
- They feel insecure in their abilities and therefore do not want to ask for feedback for fear of hearing something detrimental.

All of these reasons are valid; however, the whole principle of coaching is around improving performance and therefore coaches should lead by example.

Model for receiving feedback

We would like to thank Andrew Rea for the process that we have included in this section.

Listen
Don't interrupt whilst the feedback is in full flow, listen carefully to what is being said to you. In most circumstances it will be information that will support your development.

'Right. . . .uuummmmm. . .OK'
NOT
'I didn't!!'

Check your understanding
Make sure, after the person has finished speaking, that you understand what he or she said. Try to paraphrase it back for clarity.

'So you are saying that when I said ,'Only an idiot could have designed our Bought Ledger system' that the system designers went red and tears came to their eyes?'
NOT
'You're talking rubbish.'

Try not to be defensive
Some feedback can hurt and be painful to hear. Even positive feedback can be hard to accept and we tend to brush it off. Control your own feelings.

'Thank you. No-one has ever told me that before about my smile.'
NOT
'Flatterer!!'

Ask for examples
Your feedback giver may not be working to the rules of feedback but there is nothing to prevent you from asking for examples and for specific information to enable you to judge the quality of the feedback.

'When and how did I upset Pat?'
NOT
'Pat's always in tears.'

Choose what to do with the feedback
You can accept feedback and try to change your behaviours for the better or can totally reject the feedback and carry on as before. Here is where your judgement and feelings about the giver come into play and also what you think are that person's motives for giving you the feedback.
    Your options are:

- LISTEN and try to change.
- LISTEN and try to gather more data.
- LISTEN and ignore.

Relate to other situations and experiences
Check your memory of similar events in the past. Have others cried when you talked with them or 'got a bit annoyed'? Have others revealed more to you when

you plan interviews and use open questions? Is this feedback an isolated incident or does it fit into a pattern? If in a pattern, could things be different for you if you tried to change or not?

Check feedback with others
Go and talk with others who were at the same meeting, interview, etc and see if their observation of the facts and feelings they had matched those of your feedback giver. This is where you can check if there has been any 'dumping' on you by the giver.

Thank the giver for the feedback and let him or her know how you feel after receiving it.
It is not easy to give feedback in a constructive manner – especially negative feedback – so recognize that it might have been a painful process for the giver as well as for you, the recipient.

'Thank you for that information about my choice of language at that meeting. I feel upset that I didn't see that I had distressed some people, and didn't calm the situation at the time. I will check out your feedback with Micky who was there too and then decide what to do about the systems designers.'
NOT
'Thanks a bunch you ratbag, how many other people are you going to insult today?'

Dealing with coachee reactions to your feedback

Let's imagine that you have given your coachee some feedback relating to your observations and he or she has reacted badly – having begun by denying that what you saw is what happened, the coachee has now given you a range of excuses for it. The coachee is obviously upset and at this stage he or she is probably being defensive. So what can you do?

You should have considered this possible reaction before giving your feedback and ideally have built up a strategy for dealing with it, based upon your knowledge of this person. However, if you have not – or even if you have and your strategy is not working – the first thing that you must do is 'centre' yourself. This may sound like a very 'fluffy' term, but what it means is that you must take control of your own emotions about the situation. Remember what you are trying to achieve – what are the objectives of the coaching process? Have confidence in the quality of the feedback you are giving – your feedback is based upon facts and not inferences. Remember that, similar to an angry customer reacting to a member of staff in a shop, the coachee is not reacting to you, but to what they have heard you say or even what they have done. Don't get drawn into an argument – 'stay on the same side'.

Once you have centred yourself, consider addressing the behaviour that the coachee is exhibiting now. Move away from the activity and potential arguments of 'Yes, you did', 'No, I didn't' and tell the person what he or she is doing and the impact it is having on you and/or the feedback process. At this point you may find the following expressions useful:

- **'I note that** you seem to be upset.'
- **'It's almost as if** you think I'm picking on you.'
- **'You are** shouting at me. Please stop; I don't like it.'
- **'You seem to feel** very strongly about this. Can we talk about that? It is important to me that we don't fall out about this.'
- **'My intention was to explain** what I saw.'
- **'Tell me** how you feel/what you are thinking now.'

Having addressed the reaction to the feedback, establish with your coachee whether you can carry on now or need to meet at a later date.

Self-appraisal – the coachee's perception

The purpose of self-appraisal (self-evaluation) is to get the coachee to reflect upon his or her own performance and behaviour. While mainly we will ask coachees to do this in an objective way, an important part of the process is encouraging them to respond to their own intuitions about the situation or activity. It is difficult for any of us to be objective when faced with ourselves! So, in addition to asking them to think about what went well and what difficulties they experienced, they should also ask 'How do I feel about this?'

To a certain extent, everybody self-evaluates. The question is what people do with the results of their self-evaluation. Are they constructive or destructive? Do they ask themselves 'What can I learn from this?' and then move on or do they go over and over their 'mistakes' until they are gibbering wrecks who cannot function? The difference is on the focus – are they looking to the future, thinking about next time or are they stuck in the past? The role of the coach is to help their coachees to keep moving towards their desired outcomes.

So, how do we self-appraise?

There are many ways in which you can encourage your coachee to self-appraise; however, a simple and straightforward method involves asking a series of questions:

- What happened?
- What aspects of it were positive?
- What aspects were negative?
- Why were they positive and negative?
- What do I want to replicate next time?
- What do I want to avoid next time?
- How will I do this?

Ideally the coachee will be able to work through these questions and then discuss ideas with you, the coach. However, we all know that this is not an ideal world and you may need to ask these questions and challenge the coachee's answers during the subsequent discussion.

Another technique is to use learning logs or reflective journals. A learning log is a tool to assist reflection. Just as with a personal diary, it is rare that the coachee will be able to write notes about the activity as it is happening. However, it is vital that the coachee completes the learning log immediately on completion of the activity – the coaching plan should therefore include time for completion of the learning log.

The learning log given in Figure 10.1 is for guidance only – support coachees as they create a learning log that fits their style. Some people prefer to have a blank notebook; others prefer to use a lined pad and a folder. Another alternative is to use a Dictaphone or even a video camera to record the learning.

One suggestion is that the coachee uses a learning log *pro forma* similar to that which the coach has used for his or her observation notes – this will make it easier to discuss and compare thoughts during review meetings.

Other techniques for self-evaluation can be found in Part 3. Whichever technique you and your coachee choose, self-evaluation has to be part of the coaching plan.

Third-party feedback

We have already recommended that you do not pass on third-party feedback to your coachee. If third-party feedback is to be involved then your coaching plan should include the coachee collecting this feedback; however, you will need to discuss it at your review meetings.

Be prepared for different reactions from your coachee to this type of feedback. Imagine a scenario where the coachee thinks he or she has done well but a customer or colleague thinks the opposite – who is correct? It could be that the other person is measuring the coachee against different standards or has different expectations; in which case, neither is right or wrong. You and your

What happened?	
Key learning points:	How this experience connects with other learning:
Plan to use the learning in the future:	New learning needs now revealed:
Other points to note:	

Figure 10.1 A sample learning log

coachee need to discuss why the difference exists; look again at the facts and why the coachee thinks the experience has gone well. This is where you need to ask some probing questions about what really happened.

Planning for improved performance

This is the point where you need to pull the evidence and reflections together and ask 'What does it all mean?' within the context of what we are trying to achieve. Scientifically, this could be as simple as listing the original objectives, putting evidence next to the objectives to show where the coachee did and did not meet the criteria and noting the gaps.

In reality, it may be harder, as some of the evidence may not easily link to the objectives or there may not be sufficient evidence that the desired performance goals have been achieved. In the first instance, the implication is that the coaching plan was flawed and/or the methods chosen were inappropriate. In the second case, a lack of sufficient evidence means that there is a need to redo the task and collect more – perhaps targeted at the specific things missed the first time. In both cases, it could be a reflection on the quality of evidence – perhaps the observer missed some elements of behaviour or the coachee is not being truly honest.

When you have considered the experience from all angles and discussed why things happened the way they did then it is time to move on to action planning. You are ready to think about what needs to happen next time.

You now begin to highlight options for action. At this point you will have a list, arising from the activity and subsequent analysis, of what worked for the coachee and what did not produce the desired results. This list is a valuable asset as it tells the coachee what he or she needs to do – it provides information about how close the coachee is to achieving the coaching objectives. What you need to do now is look at all the gaps and come up with options for closing them. In addition to this you will be looking at what the coachee has done well and how this good performance can be maintained. This is then going to be turned into a plan of what the coachee will do next time he or she carries out this job or task.

The art to this stage is creativity – producing ideas, thinking 'outside the box' and looking at all the possible routes to the required outcome.

Your role as coach now is to:

- encourage creativity;
- maintain a non-judgmental attitude about the ideas;
- facilitate the coachee to produce ideas;
- offer suggestions;
- write all the ideas down.

Your job is to encourage the coachee to produce ideas and stop him or her discounting or selecting options until later. In order to do this, you must have an open mind yourself and not be thinking that there is a right or wrong answer (or if you know there is a right answer, you must allow the coachee to get to the next stage where he or she will explore the pros and cons of each option).

Hence the requirement to ask open, and sometimes challenging questions, such as:

- 'What could you do?'
- 'What needs to happen?'
- 'What didn't you do this time?'
- 'What else could you do?'
- 'What other options did you have?'
- 'If you didn't do that next time, what could you do instead?'
- 'What do you wish you had done?'

It is your role to stop the coachee coming up with one solution and deciding that that is the only way forward – selection comes later.

There may be times when coachees have no ideas – they are not happy with how they have performed but can't see options for changing their behaviour. In this situation, you want them to think about what is unsettling them; you may need to return to the evidence – 'This is what you did, what happened and how do you feel about it?' This in itself may help them identify alternative behaviours and strategies.

However, you may need to give them ideas or options – being careful not to lead them into thinking that your solution is the right one! We recommend the statements:

'One option is. . .'
or
'What would happen if you did. . .'
or
'Other people have found that. . . is effective.'

Once you have identified all the potential options for filling the gaps in performance, you and the coachee need to revise the original coaching plan with the decisions about what needs to happen next. In effect, this takes you back to Stage 3 of the coaching process (see Chapter 8), ready to repeat Stage 4 (see Chapter 9) and so on until you have achieved all the objectives. Remember to discuss how the coachee will maintain effective or good behaviour/performance.

You may have met all the development needs – in which case there will be no further performance gaps – you are now ready to end the coaching relationship.

What could go wrong

The coachee reacts badly to the feedback you give.

One reaction that a coachee may have is denial. Denial is when a person says 'That didn't happen' or 'This is not happening to me'. Delusion is sometimes easier than facing reality. A person in denial will not acknowledge that a situation exists.

A coachee may also offer excuses. This is about blaming someone or something else —'It's not my fault.' Often blame is placed on an organization rather than an individual, particularly by those individuals who do not feel that they have any formal power (authority) to change a situation.

Finally, the coachee might suffer from 'Ostrich syndrome'. This is about burying your head in the sand and hoping that, because you cannot see what is happening, it will all go away. This is different from denial because here there is some acknowledgement that something is going on.

The role of the coach is to help the coachee to face reality, even if it is difficult and unpalatable for him or her. We do this by offering evidence to the coachee about what happened and asking probing, challenging questions which do not let the coachee off the hook. When doing this, be prepared for some adverse reactions from the coachee, such as aggression, tears, silence and/or the coachee wanting to end the relationship.

Dealing with reactions to feedback

If the person disagrees constructively:

- Listen, check your facts, get additional information.
- Give the coachee time to think over your comments.
- Be prepared to change your ideas.

If the person shifts blame:

- Ask why the coachee does this.
- Listen carefully.
- Ask what help the coachee needs to give him or her confidence.
- Ask how this help can be given.

If the person loses his or her temper:

- Listen.
- Do not argue.
- Terminate the discussion and continue later.

If the person is passive and unresponsive:

- Ask why the coachee is taking this attitude.
- Give the coachee plenty of opportunity to talk.
- Watch for any interest.
- Explain and re-explain the constructive purpose of the discussion.
- Ask plenty of open questions.

New training or coaching needs come to light.

Whilst analysing how a task or experience has gone it might become apparent that the coachee has a training need, or that the coaching need originally identified is incorrect. Remember, a training need is where there is a gap in knowledge or skill, and a coaching need is where performance can be enhanced. Let's take an example of when one coaching need could become a different one. Say the coaching objectives are about being able to write a report; during the implementation stage of the process it becomes apparent that the coachee is now competent at writing reports, but has upset people whilst doing the research for the report. In this case the need is now about developing interpersonal skills and therefore a separate coaching relationship (maybe with the same coach) needs to be established, unless this was included in the original objectives.

If you identify a new training or coaching need, you have a number of options:

- Stop coaching and go into training mode, if you have the ability to do so – change your role and input the missing knowledge or skill.
- Recognize the training requirement and include it in the person's development plan for a later date, to be trained by yourself or another training resource.
- Go back to Stage 2 (see Chapter 7) and re-agree the purpose and objectives of the coaching relationship. Consider with the new purpose and objectives whether you are still the most appropriate coach for this person.

- End the coaching relationship – maybe coaching is not the right solution or perhaps the need you have now identified is not a priority for the organization.

Skills required

- listening;
- questioning;
- facilitation;
- verbal communication;
- presenting ideas;
- planning;
- analysing.

11

Stage 6: Ending the coaching relationship

A coaching relationship should have a start and end point. Ending the relationship will mean that the coach is ready to continue without your support, not necessarily that he or she has finished developing. You may continue a relationship with your coachee, especially if you are the person's line manager, but it is important to highlight the end of the coaching process so that you are clear about the purpose of future interactions.

By the end of this stage of the coaching process you should have the following outcomes:

- An evaluation of the coaching programme.
- Actions to include on your own development plan as a coach.

What you do

You only evaluate and end the relationship when all the learning objectives have been met. You are evaluating in order to assess whether you have achieved what you set out to achieve in terms of meeting the original development need. By the very nature of going through the process you will be evaluating against your objectives continually, as you progress.

Additionally you will want to find out how you did as a coach. To do this you will probably employ some of the review techniques that you encouraged your coachee to use. Tools for evaluation can be found in Part 3.

You and the coachee may choose to celebrate the end of the relationship.

What could go wrong

The coachee does not want to end the relationship.

This may be because the coachee suddenly loses his or her confidence when you say that the coaching has finished. The coachee has been performing confidently up to this point, but is now scared to continue completely alone. It may be that the coachee does not want to take final responsibility for performing the task or job and as long as the person can claim to be in a coaching relationship he or she will not have to.

You will need to use your judgement and knowledge of the individual and decide whether you are going to gradually wean him or her off the coaching sessions or stick to what you have said and withdraw totally and immediately.

Skills required

● verbal communication;
● assertiveness.

12

Third-party initiated coaching

Coaching is sometimes initiated by someone other than the coachee or the coach. In this case there are some things that you, the coach, will want to consider. These will include how much involvement the third party wants to have in the coaching process and how much you are prepared to allow. There will also be issues of confidentiality between you and the coachee and the possibility that the third party and the coachee may have different agendas.

If a third party has initiated the coaching, the coach should have a conversation with this person to establish the exact reasons for the request. The following list of questions may be helpful here:

- What makes you think that this person will benefit from coaching?
- What specific behaviours have you noticed that you would like to see changing?
- What do you want this person to be able to do better?
- What is the person not doing that you believe he or she is capable of?
- What achievements do you see this person being able to make as a result of coaching?
- What specific incidents can you describe that have led to this request for coaching?
- What have you told this person about your request for coaching?
- Why have you chosen coaching, rather than other methods of development?
- What support will you be able to give this person during the coaching period and beyond?
- What do you think the impact of any changes in this person will be on your team and on others with whom the person comes into contact? How do you plan to deal with this impact?
- What feedback are you expecting to receive from me and from the coachee?

It is important to establish whether the third person has told the coachee that he or she is being nominated for coaching. The coach should not be the one who tells the coachee that he or she needs coaching. This is the job of the third party, usually the line manager – in reality, however, the line manager may hope that you will take this on as part of the job of coaching. This is a crucial part of the process of preparing the coachee. Imagine the problems that might arise during your first contact with the coachee if that person did not know that he or she was a candidate for this type of development! It may be that the line manager does not feel able to give the coachee the feedback that is required and therefore the coach will need to do some work with the line manager before getting involved with the coachee.

Establishing the coaching contract

The coaching contract is the agreement that you have with the stakeholders. Very often this will be in writing.

Whether you are an in-house coach, or you have been commissioned as an external provider, some ethical issues may come up for you. Who are you responsible to? At one level your main responsibility is to the coachee; you will be working with the coachee on a one-to-one basis, you will be gaining his or her trust and potentially sharing confidences. On another level, when asked to coach by a third person you are in effect being contracted to complete a task by that person and therefore you are accountable to him or her. There may be things that you are told by the third party, or which you are aware of because of your role within the organization, that you cannot pass on to the coachee. *You* will need to decide what to do, probably on each occasion, but with consideration to your own values, the organizational culture/needs and the precise nature of your relationship with both coachee and third party.

These following areas would be included in a coaching contract.

Agreeing objectives

An important issue is whose objectives you will be working to. Regardless of the briefing that you receive from the third party, you will still complete all the stages of the coaching process, including analysing the coaching need and setting objectives for the programme with the coachee. Potentially, therefore, there may be some conflict or differences between what the coachee wants to achieve and what the line manager thinks the coachee should achieve. Your role is to negotiate, and perhaps mediate, between coachee and line manager until all three of you can agree on a set of objectives for the coaching programme. This sounds easy, but it could take a long time, involve a number of meetings and may even result in the cancellation of the coaching altogether! The coachee must completely buy into the coaching objectives for the process to be successful.

Feedback

The contract should establish what feedback the third party will receive. Experience suggests that line managers and other stakeholders will want feedback on how the coachee is doing. You have a responsibility to provide feedback to them; the issue is what type of feedback you will give and how much detail you will go into. This is part of your initial negotiations and all parties should agree before the coaching programme begins. The coachee must be made aware of what feedback you have promised to give to whom. One option in dealing with this situation is to encourage the coachee to give the feedback; this could be part of the learning process for the coachee and is particularly important if the third party is the line manager as the coachee should be discussing his or her progress with the line manager. There will be times when the third party still wants you to give him or her feedback; at the end of each coaching session, agree with the coachee what you will each report back on.

Support for the coachee

What support is the coachee going to get back in the workplace, both during and after the coaching programme? It is important that as the coachee makes changes in behaviour and performance, he or she is given positive encouragement and reinforcement. Equally if the coachee is focusing on specific jobs or tasks, he or she should be given the opportunity to continue to carry them out during and after the coaching. Some changes are difficult to make, especially if they concern making changes about ourselves or jobs that we have done for a long time; this change process can be helped or hindered by the way the people around us react to it. Identify the support available for the coachee whilst talking to the person who initiated the coaching, and be prepared to pass this information on to the coachee.

In summary, if a third party approaches you to provide coaching, take the following steps:

- Meet with the third party to discuss what he or she thinks are the needs, how the needs were identified and what the coachee has been told about the needs and the process to address them. This is an opportunity to find out what the third party is expecting from you and what he or she is expecting to see as a result of the coaching.
- Clarify the coaching process with the third party. Even when a manager has asked for coaching, it may be that that person doesn't really know what he or she is asking for.
- Clarify principles and ground rules for the third party's involvement in the coaching process. This includes discussing the type and content of any feedback that you will be providing for him or her.
- Discuss how the third party can support this process by creating an environment in which the coachee will feel able to change and implement his or her learning. This includes giving personal support to the individual as well as providing the opportunity for the coachee to practise – in some cases that might mean reallocating some of the coachee's tasks to other people.
- Summarize this in the coaching contract, in writing if appropriate.

13

Skills

As we have talked about the process, we have identified the different skills that you will need to use as you carry out coaching. This chapter gives a short summary of each of these skills and a few tips about how to develop them. This alone will not enable you to develop the skills to the required level, but, we hope, will offer enough for you to be able to identify your strengths and areas to include in your own development plan. (You may even want to get yourself a coach!) We have also included a section entitled Skills in the list of Further Reading at the end of the book – the publications listed there are useful if you wish to explore any of the skills in greater depth.

In this chapter we have identified skills and listed them in alphabetical order. However, we have discovered that in reality the skills overlap, sometimes even merge into each other, ie you can't use one skill without using another.

Analytical skills

You will be using analytical skills throughout the coaching process. At each stage you will have some information that you will need to make sense of in order to move you on through the process. One option is that you simply gather the information, mull it over in your brain and let conclusions seep through from your unconscious mind. The other option is to take a more systematic approach to analysis and involve your coachee. The benefits of the latter are that you are creating a structured approach and encouraging the coachee to own the analysis, enabling the coachee to do it him- or herself in the future.

Analysis is about looking at information and drawing conclusions from it. There are a number of steps that you take in carrying out analysis.

1. Collection of information.
2. Categorization of information.
3. Creating and testing hypotheses, theories and assumptions.
4. Checking hypotheses and theories and drawing final conclusions.

In the coaching relationship, most of the information that you will be analysing will come from the coachee. Some may come from third parties and possibly from task outputs/observations.

The real skill is around categorizing the information and drawing conclusions from it. A number of things may inform the categories that you choose:

- Questions such as 'What do I want to know from this information?' or 'What does this information tell me?'.
- Things that the coachee has told you about what he or she wants to achieve from the coaching.
- The objectives that you have agreed for the coaching.
- Your knowledge of the subject.

Having categorized your information, you can begin to create some hypotheses, theories or assumptions. These will generally come from looking for themes or patterns that run through the information and a number of different sources of evidence all saying the same thing.

Example 1: Your coaching topic is improving delegation. Categories might be what the coachee does well, what the coachee finds difficult and what problems arise because the coachee can't delegate.

Your hypotheses could be generated from the fact that there are more things in the 'problems' pile than in the 'finds difficult' pile. One hypothesis might be that the coachee spends little time supporting the person who has been delegated the task; another might be that the coachee feels that he or she is able to delegate, but that the organization is preventing him or her from doing so. These are the hypotheses that you would then explore further with the coachee.

Example 2: Your coaching topic is building a brick wall. Categories might be knowledge, skills and attitude.

The hypothesis will come from the information that tells you that the coachee is technically competent to build a wall, but has a limiting belief about the value of his or her work. The hypothesis is that the coaching needs to focus on the attitudinal aspects of the coachee's work. You will check out this hypothesis with the coachee before agreeing the coaching objectives.

The art of effective analysis involves remaining objective at all times. It is often easy to look at information with a foregone conclusion or to allow your experience to limit your thinking. It is therefore important to always think widely and openly about the information in front of you and try to create at least two hypotheses about what the information is telling you.

Assertiveness

Assertiveness is based on a philosophy of personal responsibility and awareness of the rights of other people. Being assertive means being honest with yourself and others. It means having the ability to say directly what it is you want, you need or you feel, but not at the expense of other people. It means having confidence in yourself and being positive while at the same time understanding other people's points of view. It means being able to behave in a rational and adult way. Being assertive means being able to negotiate and reach workable compromises. Above all, being assertive means having self-respect and respect for other people.

A coach needs to be assertive because generally this type of behaviour is the most effective way to communicate with others. The philosophies of coaching and assertiveness are closely aligned – they are both about personal responsibility and increasing confidence. In order to encourage this in others, it is important that we model this behaviour ourselves.

In order for the coachee to be able to learn, your role is to support his or her self-esteem at all times. Self-esteem means the level of belief you have in yourself and it indicates the level of self-acceptance. It is a way of measuring how worthwhile you judge yourself to be and a way of measuring your psychological well-being.

There are four broad definitions of behaviour. These are:

- passive;
- aggressive;
- passive/aggressive – manipulative;
- assertive.

When you are behaving in these ways you are likely to take on one of three roles – parent, adult or child (as described by transactional analysis).

Assertiveness takes practice. You will find that in some situations and with some people, you naturally become more passive and aggressive. Assertiveness in coaching will positively support both your relationship and the process by enabling you to have an honest and open dialogue. See Figures 13.1 and 13.2 for more information.

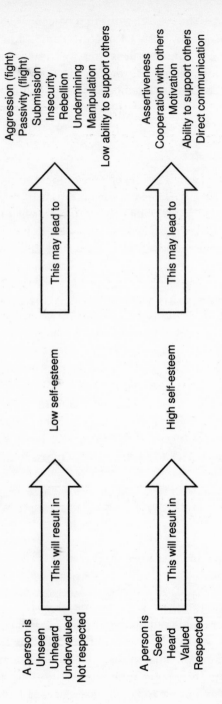

Figure 13.1 The relationship of self-esteem and assertiveness

Passive behaviour:
Keen to avoid confrontation, even at the expense of themselves.
Hope that others will know what they want, rather than communicating it.
Excessively concerned with what others may say or think about them.

Minimal eye contact.
Quiet and hesitant voice.
Rambling speech.
Defensive, shrinking posture.

Aggressive behaviour:
Keen to win, even at the expense of others.
Focus completely on their own needs.

Excessive eye contact.
Loud, blunt voice.
Threatening posture.
Invade personal space of others.
Finger wagging and pointing.
Banging fist on table.

Passive/aggressive behaviour (manipulative):
Hybrid of two behaviour types.
Respond aggressively when there is no risk of confrontation.
Often occurs when individuals wish to be assertive but lack the confidence to be so.

Minimal eye contact – looking away, rather than down.
Sighs impatiently.
Is 'tight-lipped'.
Uses 'I don't believe it' expressions.
Closed posture.

Assertive behaviour:
Keen to stand up for own rights, while always considering those of others.
Body language supports what they are saying.
Controlled, moderate, neutral voice tone.
Open posture.

The child ego-state.
Someone else knows better than I do.
I need to be parented.

Blames self.
Avoids issues.
Seeks permission of others.
Backs down easily.
Generates sympathy for self.

The parent ego-state.
I know better than others.
I will take the role of controlling, critical parent.

Blames others.
Makes personal, not constructive, criticism.
Interrupts others.
Authoritarian.
Gives orders, rather than makes requests.

A controlling and critical parent, pretending to be nurturing.
The underlying belief is that I know better than others,
but will not say so outright.

Indirect responses.
Sarcastic. Uses barbed humour.
Moans about things, sometimes
within earshot of those they are talking about.
Manipulates others to benefit self.

The adult ego-state.
Each person has something of value
to contribute. All views should be heard.
I value myself and others.
Actively listens.
Respectful of others.
Generates workable compromise.
Seeks solutions.
Open about their own views, feelings and opinions.
Direct, not abrupt.
Stands by own opinions, but prepared to change them.

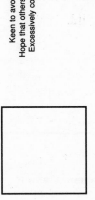

Figure 13.2 The relationship of assertiveness to parent-adult-child ego states

Conflict management

The Chinese symbol for conflict combines two symbols – one of which is danger, the other opportunity. The way you deal with conflict will decide which way it goes.

Here are some reasons why you might get into a conflict situation with your coachee:

- You give the coachee some feedback which he or she is not ready or willing to hear and/or you do it in a clumsy or inappropriate way.
- One of you suggests something that the other disagrees with.
- The coachee is not keeping to the ground rules that you laid down together.
- One of you feels that the coaching is finished, but the other does not.

All these situations describe times when you and your coachee are on opposing sides of an argument. A conflict arises when one or other of you is not willing to negotiate or talk about the fact that there is a disagreement.

There is a useful model which helps to look at the source of conflict. Most conflicts have three levels at which they operate. The first level is the 'issue' level; this is what the conflict or disagreement is actually about, eg washing up being left in the sink or someone being late for meetings you've arranged. The second level is the 'relationship' level; this is what the conflict is *really* about – this is also the level that people usually get emotional about. For example, being late for a meeting is about not respecting you, or what the people in the meeting are doing, enough to turn up on time. This is the level that often does not get discussed in conflicts – we focus on the issue rather than admit our feelings or concerns about the relationship. The problem is that because you do not talk about the relationship, the other person may not understand why there is a difficulty. The third level is 'source' – the psychology of why things have the impact on us that they do. Because this can be rooted in our childhood or past experiences, we tend to encourage people to stay away from this area, unless trained to deal with these types of issues.

This means that, in terms of dealing with conflict, you need to have a discussion with the coachee at the relationship level, not just the issue level.

If you find yourself in a conflict situation:

- Deal with the situation immediately. Do not let it fester.
- Deal with your own emotions about the situation. Part of this is about acknowledging what your emotions are and why they have come about.

- Get a perspective on the situation, perhaps by taking a step back and looking at it objectively.
- Talk to the coachee, while remaining calm and assertive. Point out the behaviour that is causing a problem and discuss ways in which the problem can be resolved. Acknowledge the coachee's emotions about the conflict.
- Try to reach a mutually acceptable solution, even if that is agreeing to differ.
- If emotions are running too high to enable you to reach a solution, you may have to call the meeting to a close.

Facilitation

The word facilitation derives from the Latin word *facilis*, meaning 'to make easy'. So in facilitating the coaching process you are making it as easy as possible for the coachee to develop.

Within an interaction with another person, the facilitator needs to be aware of what is happening at different levels, usually expressed as:

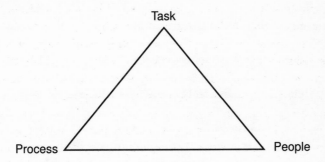

Figure 13.3 Different levels of an interaction

TASK – is the subject of the coaching – the reason for you and the coachee being together.

PROCESS – is how something is happening; this is the actual coaching process. The coach will need to listen and observe carefully, being aware of the processes and their impact.

PEOPLE – is the coach and coachee relationship. You may also need to think about relationships with third parties, either stakeholders or other people involved in the task. As the coach, you have the prime responsibility for facilitating the relationship to ensure that the task and process take place.

As a facilitator, you will need to work on all three levels at any one time to ensure that your work with the coachee is effective and productive.

An effective facilitator:

- keeps focused on the task;
- follows the process;
- uses listening, observing and questioning skills at appropriate times;
- challenges perceptions and ideas in a supportive manner;
- maintains objectivity;
- helps others identify options;
- builds useful relationships that work;
- helps draw conclusions about the way forward.

A facilitator basically draws out more than he or she puts in; this means helping the other person access their full potential in the coaching subject area.

Influencing

Consider the following dictionary definitions:

'Influence – the power of producing an effect, especially unobtrusively; the effect of power exerted; a person exercising such power; a spiritual influx'.
'Influential – effectively active in bringing something about'.

In his book *Working with Emotional Intelligence*, Goleman (1999) includes influence within our social competence (determining how we handle relationships). He defines influence as 'wielding effective tactics for persuasion', and explains that people with this competence:

- are skilled at winning people over;
- fine-tune presentations to appeal to the listener;
- use complex strategies like indirect influence to build consensus and support;
- orchestrate dramatic events to effectively make a point.

When you are influencing someone, you are attempting to alter his or her perceptions, views, beliefs, attitudes etc. This means helping the person to make sense of your views, think them through, accept them and then act upon them. It therefore relies upon the way you communicate with that person.

Influencing others involves finding a communication style that works with the other person, so that they are more likely to hear and understand you. Your coachee is more likely to be influenced by you if he or she can relate to what you are saying; the only way you are going to be able to say something that your coachee can relate to, is if you have listened to him or her and attempted to understand his or her situation.

People with influence have presence. They behave confidently, which adds to their credibility in the eyes of others. If you use the other skills within this section, you are likely to be an effective influencer.

In the coaching relationship, as the coach you probably have the balance of power: either because of your position in the organization or because of the way the coachee views you. Positional power has limited use in the coaching relationship; best results are achieved by using your personal skills to influence the coachee.

Listening

The diagram below illustrates what we often think it is like when we talk to someone.

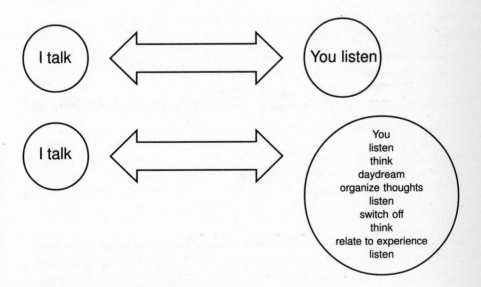

Figure 13.4 The process of listening

Hearing is only the first part of listening – the physical part when your ears **sense** sound waves. There are three other equally important parts. There's the **interpretation** of what was heard that leads to understanding, or misunderstanding. Then comes the **evaluation** stage when you weigh the information and decide how you'll use it. Finally, based on what you heard and how you evaluated it, you react. That's listening.

Tests have shown that immediately after listening to a 10-minute oral presentation, the average listener has heard, understood, properly evaluated and retained approximately half of what was said. And within 48 hours, that drops off another 50 per cent to a final 25 per cent level of effectiveness – in other words, we quite often comprehend and retain only one-quarter of what was said.

10 keys to effective listening

These keys, shown in Figure 13.5, provide a positive guide to better listening. In fact, they are at the heart of developing better listening habits that could last a lifetime.

In order to *really* listen to another person, use the following points as guidelines:

- Concentrate on the other person. Try to give him or her 100 per cent of your attention. If you feel that you need to take notes, explain what you are doing and why.
- Encourage the other person to feel comfortable with you and to want to speak to you. Nod and smile appropriately, ask constructive and relevant questions that are based upon what you have heard.
- Respond to the other person as detailed above and demonstrate that you have been listening by reflecting back what you are hearing. Use phrases like:'What I am hearing is. . .', 'You seem to be saying that. . .', 'I sense that you. . .' and so on.
- Non-verbal signals will tell the other person whether you are listening.
- Eye contact will show that you are interested in the other person. Do not stare, but maintain eye contact for the majority of the time that you are in discussion.
- Body language such as that described earlier will help the other person to know that you are listening. You should also adopt an open, interested position. Turning away from the person or folding your arms will send messages of disapproval and may cause the person to 'dry up'.

10 Keys to Effective Listening	The Poor Listener	The Effective Listener
1. Find areas of interest	Tunes out dry subjects	Opportunist; asks 'what's in it for me?'
2. Judge content, not delivery	Tunes out if delivery is poor	Judges content, skips over delivery errors
3. Hold your fire	Tends to enter into argument	Doesn't judge until comprehension is complete
4. Listen for ideas	Listens for facts	Listens for central themes
5. Be flexible	Takes intensive notes using only one system	Takes fewer notes
6. Work at listening	Shows no energy output. Fakes attention	Works hard, exhibits active body state
7. Resist distractions	Is easily distracted	Fights or avoids distractions, tolerates bad habits, knows how to concentrate
8. Exercise your mind	Resists difficult material; seeks light, recreational material	Uses heavier material as exercise for the mind
9. Keep your mind open	Reacts to emotional words	Interprets colour words; does not get hung up on them
10. Think about the facts, it is faster than speech	Tends to daydream with slow speakers	Challenges, anticipates, mentally summarizes, weighs the evidence, listens between the lines to voice tone

Figure 13.5 10 Keys to effective listening

- Speech rhythm/tone/silence all have an effect on the way in which people feel about communicating with you. If, when you speak, you do so in a hurried and rushed fashion, then the other person will feel as if you do not have the time to listen to him or her. Your tone of voice can either pass on the message that you are listening or that you are impatient and wish to move the conversation on. Silence can be used very effectively to prompt the other person to speak to you.
- We are often afraid of silences and therefore try to fill them with conversation; this temptation is best avoided.
- Ask questions relating to what you have been told. This will assist in clarifying and in encouraging the coachee to give you further details.

- Try to remain objective and neutral as you are listening – avoid relating your own experiences to those that you are hearing about – 'I remember when a similar thing happened to me. . .' will not be helpful when you are focusing your attention on the speaker and his or her experience.
- Listen for recurring themes in what the person is saying to you. Does the speaker repeat the same phrase? Does he or she refer back to a specific situation? Ask questions relating to any themes that you are hearing.
- Recap on what you have heard the speaker say to you at the end of each session.

Reflection and paraphrasing

Reflection and paraphrasing are methods of feeding back to the speaker the information that you have just been given. When you reflect back what someone has been telling you, you relay to him or her the **whole** of the message that you have just received. The whole of the message (as indicated previously) comes not only from the words that the speaker is using, but also from his or her tone of voice and body language.

To paraphrase is to express what you have been told in other words. Paraphrasing is a useful tool when you wish to check your understanding of what the speaker is telling you. For example, the speaker may be describing a particular procedure to you. When you paraphrase what you have been told you will describe the procedure to the speaker, but using your own words to explain your understanding of what you have been told.

In summary, an effective coaching session will have a balance of talking and listening – the coachee will do most of the talking, the coach will do most of the listening.

Observation

'You have seen, but not observed' Sherlock Holmes said to Dr Watson. Observation is a skill which can be practised – it involves looking at the whole picture and the parts of the picture from a variety of different angles and perspectives so that we can draw various conclusions from what we have seen.

The starting point for observation is to have a clear view of what you are trying to accomplish. What do you need to look for in order to achieve the coaching objectives? What information are you trying to gather? If there are laid down standards for the way in which a task is to be completed, you should always take this into account when carrying out your observation.

Treat every observation as a separate event – even if you are observing a task that you have seen several times before. If you don't do this, the danger is that you may become complacent and assume that you are seeing something that you aren't. Every situation is unique and therefore there will be differences from the last time the task was carried out – focus on what you are seeing this time and what you can learn from it. 'Make the familiar strange and the strange familiar' (Gordon, in his 1973 book *Synectics*). To help you with this ask yourself some questions to help generate new insights, eg 'How will I explain what I am seeing to the coachee?', 'What is the coachee doing differently this time?', 'What does the coachee look comfortable or uncomfortable doing?', 'What am I actually seeing here?'.

In order to improve your observation skills, try watching the same piece of video tape over and over again in order to spot differences or go to a large shopping centre and do some people-watching – what do you see? Do you see men, women and children or do you also see many individuals?

When observing, if you are observing a long task, you may find your mind wandering. This is normal! Ways in which to minimize this include writing notes about what you are seeing, clearing your mind by saying to yourself 'Focus', 'Pay attention' or physically changing your position.

There are a number of pitfalls that you may face while observing – based on the fact that we are all human beings and we all have our own biases and preferences. Each of the following 'effects' is caused by a different bias.

Primacy and recency effect

This is where you remember what you saw at the start and end of the observation, but forget what went on in the middle. Timing your note-taking will help you with this.

Most significant events effect

This effect occurs when you base your assessment of the coachee's performance upon one or two significant events that take place during the period of your observation, rather than the whole performance. Taking comprehensive notes across the whole period of the observation will help lessen this effect.

Halo effect

This is where one good behaviour or action influences you into believing that the person you are observing is a saint, ie the coachee can do no wrong and everything has gone perfectly. Having clear criteria for your observation and maintaining your objectivity will lessen the chances of this.

Stereotyping

This is where your impression of the coachee, based upon your general observations about 'this type of person', colours your view on what happens. If you have already made up your mind that the coachee is good or bad at something you will only observe behaviour that reinforces that view. It is important when observing that you note both positive and negative behaviours and also that you try to discover any of your personal biases before the observation session. Another way of lessening the impact of this is by noting what you saw, rather than making a judgement about it.

Central tendency

This effect occurs when you are using a rating scale against which to assess the performance of the coachee. Rather than give a rating at either end of the scale, you may be tempted to rate the coachee at the middle. Your motivation here may be that you do not want to give the coachee difficult feedback or that you do not want the coachee to become complacent about his or her performance. It may also mean that you are not assessing the coachee against the appropriate scale. Whatever the reason for this effect, it can be overcome by making notes about the reasons for your ratings and/or by avoiding assessment against a rating scale.

Leniency/severity effect

This occurs when the observer is not fully objective about the coachee's performance, but judges the performance too kindly or too harshly. In order to keep this effect to a minimum, always bear in mind your reasons for observing the coachee, make notes of what you are actually seeing and hearing and remind yourself that you are attempting to be an impartial observer in order to give objective feedback to your coachee.

Cloning effect

When a coach has very fixed ideas about the way in which a task should be carried out, he or she is in danger of exhibiting the cloning effect – this is where the coach judges the coachee only in relation to the coach's own way of doing things. One of the best ways to avoid this effect is to discuss what you will be looking for before the observation takes place and to agree the standards with the coachee, based upon what he or she wants to improve and the way in which he or she wants to do this.

Planning and prioritizing

Planning skills are about identifying what you want to do and deciding, in small steps, how you are going to do it. The skill of planning is breaking down a task into key steps, putting them in the right order and then allocating time and other resources for each step. Successful planning involves:

- Identifying the overall aim or goal – where do I want to go?
- Writing outcome or success statements – how will I know when I have got where I want to go; what will it look and sound like?
- Identifying what actions I need to take – how will I get there?
- Prioritizing the actions required – what do I need in order to take each action? What equipment, money, time or people are required? Which actions must I take first?
- Reviewing priorities within the plan based on resources needed, which might involve reordering the steps based on availability of resources.
- Deciding how I will review my plan, both during and after implementation.

The priority of action steps will be influenced by dependencies, ie whether one thing needs to happen in order for another to take place. The other traditional way of prioritizing actions is by assessing their urgency and their importance: urgent actions are things that need to happen now, or within an immediate time frame, in order for the effect of that action to be valid. If an urgent action is not taken at the point of it being urgent, it is unlikely that you will need to take it at all. You might need to take a larger but different action, or not do anything because the moment is lost. Importance is measured in terms of the impact of the action, how vital it is to the achievement of the goal. Therefore, all tasks or actions can be viewed as being:

- urgent and important;
- urgent and not important;
- important and not urgent;
- not important and not urgent.

As a coach, you need planning skills in a number of ways. These include:

- fitting coaching time into your diary and around other responsibilities that you have;
- planning the coaching programme with your coachee;
- planning each individual coaching session.

The coachee needs to do the same planning; and sometimes your plans, and the priority level you have given to actions, may not match the coachee's. There may be times when, in the greater scheme of your life, attending the coaching session is not as important or urgent as other things; however, remember that if you decide to move the coaching session, this may adversely impact your relationship with the coachee. This isn't to say that you must never move a coaching session, only that this needs discussion and explanation.

All plans need to be flexible, in order to take account of the unknown or the unexpected. You can achieve this by building in contingency (or buffer zones), and by reviewing plans regularly with your coachee. Particularly check out if you have missed any action points that now need to be included, and that your coachee is comfortable with any deviation from the original plan.

At the start of each coaching session, you will agree a broad plan for the time you have with your coachee; as the coach it is your role to ensure that time is managed according to the plan, and if you deviate from the plan, you bring it back on course or agree a new plan.

Presenting ideas and information

People who are good at presenting their ideas and other information follow a systematic approach:

1. They consider what they want to present and why.
2. They gather their thoughts and/or information about what they want to say.
3. They put the information into a logical order – based on their audience's needs rather than their own.
4. When presenting the information, they begin by explaining why they are passing this information on and explaining the main points.
5. They support their main points with detail which will help the audience understand.

6. They observe their audience and make a judgement about the audience's reaction and level of understanding.
7. They ask for questions or comments and deal with these.
8. Finally they summarize the main points again.

The key is about considering how the people in the audience need to receive information; what words they will understand, whether it is better to present verbally or in writing, whether they will read text or prefer bullet points, what additional information they might need in order to put the information in context. Also consider how much time they might need to reflect on the information.

In the coaching context this applies to exploring ideas and concepts with your coachee, as well as when you are having discussions with stakeholders.

Questioning

The purpose of using questions is generally to encourage another person to provide you with information. In coaching situations there is an additional purpose for which questions may be used and that is to encourage the coachee to think about something.

Questions should be:

Simple – words used should be easily understood.

Short – longwinded questions may be misinterpreted.

Questions should be put:

Logically – they are less confusing in a logical sequence.

Singly – put one question or make one point at a time.

There are different types of questions, which have different purposes.

Open questions

Open questions are used when you wish to encourage the other person to talk to you and in doing so offer large amounts of information about the subject. This type of question is also used when you want the person to think widely around an issue or topic.

Famously, open questions begin with Kipling's 'Six Serving Men'; we prefer 'The Magnificent Seven':

Who?
What?
Where?
When?
How?
Which?
Why?

As a result of asking an open question, your full attention is necessary and you will need to observe, listen to and check everything in order to truly understand what you are being told.

There are other words that are not questioning words which can be used to elicit information such as 'Explain. . .', 'Tell me. . .', 'I'm interested in knowing about. . .' and 'Talk to me about. . .'.

Closed or narrow questions

These are questions that invite only a short, confined or even one word reply. They often restrict the information obtained to within the wording of the question. To most closed questions, there is a right or wrong answer. Many people frown on closed questions, but they do have their uses. They are useful when:

- seeking a 'Yes' or 'No' answer;
- selecting between alternatives;
- checking identity;
- clarifying a point.

Examples of closed questions are those starting with:

- Are you. . . ?
- Did you. . . ?
- Was it. . . ?
- Can you. . . ?

Leading questions

As a rule, in coaching, you should avoid using questions that may suggest the answer in their wording, that is, leading questions. For example, 'Did it fail because you need more practice?'. Coachees may give the expected answer just to be helpful, because they are confused or because they are frightened. They may believe that you know more about a subject than they do and feel unsure or foolish to contradict you. Leading questions may easily put information in their minds about things that they do not know for themselves, or produce ideas they have not previously formulated. However, leading questions can be useful to summarize or confirm information, eg 'So what you are saying is. . .?'.

Echoing

This is the process of repeating a phrase or the last few words of a reply. Its effect is to act like a question to prompt elaboration of a specific point and invite the other person to continue speaking about the subject.

Echoing can be particularly effective when a person who has been talking freely, stops speaking. Using echoing shows that you are listening and encourages the person to continue.

Select relevant phrases or words and do not overuse this technique. Mindless repeating of words and overuse will have the opposite effect to what you intended and can show that you are not really listening.

You should take care that any emphasis you place on words repeated does not unintentionally indicate any judgmental feelings about the other person.

Use of silence

Whilst not strictly a question, silence can be used supportively or to prompt a reluctant person to speak.

Silence can feel uncomfortable for both people: there seems a natural urge to fill pauses or gaps. However, you can learn to use silence. The selective use of silence can be a powerful tool to prompt a person to speak. When a natural break seems right, a speaker will look at the listener and pause to allow the other to speak. By using an encouraging gesture and not speaking, the listener invites the person to continue. You should allow both the other person and yourself space and thinking time. You both can then assimilate information and formulate questions or replies. Breaking eye contact may encourage this to occur. When people concentrate hard they remain silent and normally focus on a neutral space such as the floor or the ceiling. Do not interrupt this process and you may obtain that extra piece of information.

In summary, here is a process for getting good information from other people:

- Be aware of the purpose of your discussion and use this awareness to help you focus it on the information that you need.
- Use open questions to expand the discussion.
- When you are looking for specific information, or when you wish to confirm your understanding, use closed questions.
- Use your body language and tone of voice to encourage the conversation.
- Check that what you have heard is what the person meant.
- Summarize your understanding of what you have heard.

Rapport building

Rapport is built with other people when they feel as if you understand their view of the world and have respect for it. In neuro-linguistic programming (NLP) there are a number of ideas for developing rapport. Let's look at some factors that will aid the building of rapport.

Effective non-verbal communication

As a coach your non-verbal communication will be the key factor in ensuring that rapport is built with the coachee. Excellent communicators build rapport by paying conscious attention to the use of body language, tone of voice and facial expressions. Rapport may be built by matching the following areas with the interviewee:

- Posture. The position of the body, the legs and feet and weight distribution. The position of the arms, hands and fingers. The way in which the shoulders are held. The inclination of the head.
- Expression. The direction and movement of the eyes.
- Breathing. The rate of breathing and position of breathing, ie chest or abdomen.
- Movement. This refers to the pace at which the other person moves and the rhythm of their movements.
- Voice. Pace, volume, pitch, tone and type of words that are used.
- Language patterns. The use of language that is visual ('I see', 'I look at it this way'), auditory ('I hear', 'It sounds like') or feelings-based ('I feel', 'The impact of this is. . .').

Matching these areas in a subtle way gives the message to the coachee that you are like them, that you understand 'where he or she is coming from' and in turn this will help the interviewee to relax and open up to your questioning.

A person-centred approach

In building rapport with your coachee you must always bear in mind that you are dealing with another human being, an individual who has his or her own needs, wants and experiences.

Maslow identified, in *Motivation and Personality* (1954), that we all have a set of basic human needs:

- Physiological stability. The need for sufficient food, water and oxygen.
- Safety and security. The need for shelter.
- Love and belonging. The need for companionship.
- Esteem, competence and prestige. The need for recognition and achievement.
- Self-actualization. The need to become what one is capable of becoming.

When coaching, it is important to consider the lower level needs such as food, water, temperature etc since it is these things that may distract both coach and coachee. If either party is hungry, thirsty or requires a 'comfort break', the focus will not be on the process.

Equally the coach must bear in mind the higher level needs. The coachee will wish to feel accepted and respected at all times – without this the individual will not be able to consider his or her development needs and how these may be met. These needs must be satisfied if the individual is to feel comfortable enough to give information honestly and openly.

A successful coach will adopt an attitude of empathy, acceptance, respect and interest towards the coachee. This attitude will be communicated in the ways already discussed and will encourage the coachee to respond positively.

One of the most important parts of the person-centred approach is the ability to adopt what was termed by Carl Rogers 'unconditional positive regard'. This is about treating each individual as a valuable human being, whose experiences are valid and accepted. It is also about recognizing that everybody has different views of the world; a group of 10 people who have watched exactly the same play will all have very different recollections and ideas about what they have seen.

When considering different views and experiences, objectivity will be key. A phrase which is worth remembering in trying to maintain objectivity is 'not right or wrong, only different'.

Using and interpreting non-verbal communication

Our bodies, through posture, gesture and facial expression, are constantly sending messages to others. Most of us interpret non-verbal communication on an intuitive level. Body language can support or discount your verbal communication and therefore it is important for coaches to think about both their own, and their coachee's, non-verbal signals. Be wary, however, that movements and gestures sometimes have straightforward physical explanations and it is possible to over analyse everything you see the other person doing, eg someone who is scratching her nose may simply have an itch, rather than be telling a lie.

Effective body language for you as a coach includes:

- Facing the person in a way which is not confrontational.
- Maintaining an open and receptive posture.
- Finding a comfortable seating arrangement that respects the other person's personal space, but enables you to have an open conversation.
- Taking care with your appearance and dressing in a way which is appropriate for your coachee.
- Being aware of your tone of voice and using variety and contrast to enhance your messages. This includes lowering your voice to emphasize important points.
- Matching and mirroring the body language of the speaker without directly copying.
- Showing enthusiasm and sincerity using eye contact, gestures and tone of voice.
- Being aware of facial movements such as smiling, grimacing or frowning. Even small movements such as a raised eyebrow will cause others to make an interpretation of what you are thinking.

When interpreting the coachee's body language:

- Be aware that the same signal may have a variety of different meanings.
- Treat every element of body language as a message. Consider each element and look for any themes or patterns – it is difficult to properly read a single event, but a cluster of signals may provide you with a more accurate picture.
- If you are making an interpretation of any non-verbal communication, it is always worth checking that you have made the right one.

Part 2

Case studies

Case studies

In this part of the book you will find a series of case studies that we have gathered from individuals who have coached and who have been coached. These case studies give examples of different processes of coaching and different situations in which coaching has been used.

Within most of the coach case studies you will find the following:

- Some detail about the background of the coach, the situation in which coaching took place and how the coach learnt his or her coaching skills.
- A description of the process that was followed.
- Positive aspects of using the process.
- Challenges that were faced during the coaching relationship.
- What the coach learnt during the process.
- Top tips for other coaches.
- Advice and ideas for coachees.
- Some final words.
- In some instances, our comments are also given.

Use these case studies to help you formulate your own ideas about how you will use coaching. Add your own comments to ours. Compare the processes used with the one we have offered in Part 1 (see Chapter 3) and learn what you can from the experiences of others.

The coachee case studies will give you some insight about what coaching feels like when you are 'on the receiving end'. Use the experiences of the coachees to help you consider what does and does not work. Look at coaching from the other side of the relationship and use this to help you build empathy with your own coachees.

If you have any case studies that you would like to share with us, we may be able to use them in future editions of this book.

Coaching a partner in a national law firm

Geoff Coughlin

Background

Geoff Coughlin is a Director of Emphasis on Skills Ltd. His company offers tailor-made training and development in business skills. Before starting Emphasis on Skills, Geoff worked as a management and trainer development officer within public service and for an international charity. He has many years experience as a trainer, in areas including course-based learning, coaching and creation of flexible learning packages.

The situation

On this occasion, he was approached by the HR manager of a large national law firm, to coach one of the partners. This partner had development needs around planning, personal organization and influencing others. The following objectives were agreed for the coaching programme:

Programme aim

To help you build greater confidence in what you do and work in a more organized and effective way.

By the end of this session you will be able to:

- Define the role.
  - Clearly see the extent and nature of your role as you experience it in the real world and link this to exactly what you require, what your team needs and to the needs of the firm.
  - Make adjustments to any aspect of your role as you consider necessary.
- Plan systematically.

- Plan systematically any task or project you undertake establishing clear criteria for success.
- Improve personal organization.
- Prioritize and delegate work effectively within your team.
- Become more organized in the way you tackle your everyday work.
- Measure performance.
    - Use the review technique [see details below and in Part 3] to systematically review anything you do.
    - Establish exactly what has and has not gone well, and why.
    - Create an ongoing action plan for future activity.
- Influence others.
    - Use the 'Push–Pull' influencing strategy in a variety of areas of your work (link to 'Communicating achievements' below).
- Motivate the team.
    - Know what motivates your team and the practical part you play in this.
    - Give constructive feedback to team members using a four-stage method that works.
    - Come across as open-minded and an active leader of your department.
- Handle people assertively.
    - Use the Assertive Principles in your dealings with others.
    - Get you point across firmly and fairly, but not at the expense of others.
- Communicate achievements.
    - 'Celebrate' your success and that of your team with those who need to hear about it.
    - Ensure that the right people know of your achievements and be able to influence them positively.
    - Consider reward and use of praise within the team.

The process

Initially, the coachee met with the HR manager to discuss her development needs. Together they decided that coaching was the best solution based on the seniority of the coachee. Once the HR manager had identified the needs in broad terms, Geoff was asked to meet with the coachee for an exploratory meeting. The purpose of this meeting was to discuss specific needs and establish if there was a 'good personality fit'. During this meeting, they agreed key areas to be covered and what the objectives for each would be.

Also at this meeting, they agreed the coaching plan: two half-day sessions, to be run in a private meeting room on the client premises. Pre-session reading and work was included, to ensure that the coachee had underpinning knowledge, and that the coaching sessions would focus on application of skills and knowledge. A key part of the Emphasis on Skills approach is the offer of 24-hour telephone and e-mail support; this was accepted by the coachee.

This initial meeting was followed by lunch at a local restaurant, which gave both the coach and the coachee the opportunity to get to know each other better, resulting in a better rapport and stronger trust.

The first discussion session was four weeks after the initial meeting; there was a further four weeks between the first and second meetings. The meetings consisted of reflecting on how the coachee had performed certain tasks, and Geoff used the review technique to structure the meetings:

What went well? Why and how? What would you do next time?
What didn't go well? Why and how? What would you do next time?

During the coaching relationship, the 24-hour support link was used only once; the coachee said that she felt very secure and supported by having access to this.

Challenges faced

Geoff noted two challenges for himself as the coach in this situation.

The first challenge was finding the right medium in terms of confidentiality between the coachee and HR manager. Geoff and the coachee agreed ground rules and, specifically, included one that stated he would 'not discuss or give feedback on any specific information/politics/disclosure from coaching sessions to the HR manager'. It was helpful that Geoff had worked for the HR manager previously, and that they had established their own working relationship. The role of the HR manager was to:

- Give the initial brief.
- Agree fees.
- Check that the initial meeting had been successful.
- Confirm that the objectives had been met at the end.
- Ask if further sessions were required (they weren't).

The second challenge, as a consultant, was trying to understand the culture and politics that existed within the law firm. Geoff reduced the impact of his lack of knowledge about the company by asking a lot of questions and exploring why options would or would not work given the culture of the company. Emphasis on Skills do much work within the legal profession, and this general awareness of how law firms worked assisted with understanding the culture and environment that the coachee worked in.

The outcome of the coaching was that all the objectives were met in full over the two sessions, and the partner felt both more confident and in control after the coaching.

Learning

From this experience, Geoff felt that he had learnt that:

● There is a need for total trust between the coachee and the coach.
● The coachee needs to hear that the coach has integrity, a good track record and a high level of knowledge in the subject areas being worked on.
● As a coach, you must be confident that you are not going to be undermined by the HR manager or others within the organization; the coaching contract is essential so that your efforts are supported.

Top tips

● Know your subject matter.
● Draw heavily on your own experience/expertise.
● Get to know the culture of the organization your coachee is from – talk to people from all levels if you can.
● Get a thorough briefing from your contact at the organization before meeting with the coachee.
● Be honest about how long you need to provide the support your coachee requires.
● Work on building trust and a positive relationship with the coachee.
● Agree the coaching contract with the coachee and any third party stakeholders.

Final words

Coaching for individual learners is crucial to individuals being able to apply new learning back in their workplace. Ideally this coaching should be provided by the line managers in the main, and by external coaches for senior and middle managers where appropriate, where preferred by an individual or when direct support for senior managers is not forthcoming. Good training can be greatly enhanced by good coaching back in the workplace.

Authors' comments

This is a good example of third–party initiated coaching. We have left in the objectives for this coaching programme as an example of the type of objectives that you might write.

Initially, when we read this case study, we felt that there were a lot of objectives to achieve in two sessions. We note, however, that the programme was successful and that the coachee felt that she had achieved her desired outcome. This illustrates the importance of working to the coachee's agenda. Coaching is about moving the coachee forward by the amount that he or she wants to move and it would be a mistake to look at the topics and apportion time required in this way. This also shows how much more can be achieved through coaching, as opposed to attendance on training courses.

The Scout Association

Debbie Ladds

Background

Debbie Ladds is Assistant Director of Programme and Development for The Scout Association. She manages a team of people employed by the Association, as well as supporting volunteer members.

The situation

Debbie identified three different situations when she had coached individuals:

- Support of a colleague at the same level as herself in managing poor performance.
- Helping someone run a week's residential course for volunteers, and especially deal with group dynamics within the course training team.
- Helping a member of her own staff with low self-esteem.

The process

In all the examples above, Debbie employed the same approach. The first step was to identify the problem and the need for coaching. In some of the examples the individuals concerned asked for help; in one case, Debbie identified the need herself.

Once the need for coaching had been identified, Debbie discussed with her coachees the issues, reflecting on what they were doing and how they could do it differently. She then encouraged them to find solutions that might work. If Debbie felt that their suggested solutions might be unhelpful, she explored other options with them and spent time looking at the possible consequences of their actions. Once they had jointly agreed some options, she encouraged them to 'give it a try'.

After they had tried their plan, Debbie met with them to review how it went. This review process covered:

- What has been learnt?
- What has changed?
- What has stayed the same?
- What was the result of the coachee's action?

The process was repeated until the coachee felt able to carry on without the support.

Positive aspects of this approach

As you work through the various stages as many times as you need to, you can see someone learn and observe the improvement in their performance, which is very rewarding. This approach is one which can be adopted in different situations and is supportive, rather than dominant.

Challenges faced

Finding time for the process was a challenge for both the coach and the coachee. The issue needs to be a priority for the coachee otherwise he or she won't find the time to talk about it or change his or her performance. As a coach, when asked to help, there is a potential problem if you don't have the time to give – it is unhelpful to start the process and leave the coachee halfway through.

Another challenge is realizing that you are not the coachee and that you need to find solutions that will work for that person, not for you!

Learning

From her coaching experience Debbie learnt that sometimes you might need to actually see the person carry out the task you are discussing, rather than just to rely on their interpretation of what happens.

She also discovered that coaching can be very rewarding. This may be because it is real and solution orientated. It is important, however, that coachees want to undertake the coaching, rather than it being forced on them.

Debbie also learnt that coaching is time consuming and, sometimes, when it happens it is dominated by the urgency as defined by the coachee.

Top tips

- Agree a contract with coachees – formally or informally – about what they want you to do and how you will operate.
- Establish the confidentiality rules in the relationship so that they trust you.
- Create an open and honest communication style so that you are able to tell them when they have 'got it wrong' or 'could do better'.
- Be positive.
- Enjoy it!

Advice for the coachee

- Ask for help or support if you think you would benefit from it.
- Be prepared to review how you do things.
- Choose a coach that you respect, can talk to and are willing to listen to.
- Be prepared to reflect on learning (see Kolb's learning cycle).

Final thoughts

'It's worth the effort and can make a real difference to those involved.'

Authors' comments

This case study touches on the issue of finding time to coach. It is a valuable reminder to us that coaching requires dedicated time. It also emphasizes how much the coach can learn through the process.

Coaching for sales managers and their teams

Tony Latimer

Background and situation

Tony Latimer coaches sales managers and their teams following skills workshops. He calls this 'guided implementation'.

The process

Tony's approach to coaching consists of:

- clearly positioning the purpose and intent of the sessions;
- defining the present;
- identifying the desired future;
- helping coachees to get to their future.

The main purpose of the coaching sessions is to help individuals to apply the skills learnt during training; Tony has found, however, that the coach has to 'deal with lots of other issues if they exist' in order to help coachees implement their learning.

Whilst Tony uses this process, he fundamentally believes that you have to 'go where the coachee needs to', and to do this he uses non-judgemental listening with selective questioning.

Positive aspects of this approach

Allowing coachees to talk about what they want or need to enables them to work on wider issues and potential blocks to implementation of their new skills. Everyone needs someone to talk to, but few get the opportunity. Tony says there are an 'amazing number of people who comment afterwards that they have never in xx years told anyone this stuff'.

Challenges faced

Tony's challenges were: overcoming years of conditioning to give people answers and to judge them; emptying the mind and trusting the process.

Learning

Tony learnt how to become less judgemental and not to give way to the temptation to lecture or give answers from his own perspective. He also learnt that emotional moments will happen and that it is important not to react to them.

Top tips

- Get formal training in a process.
- Try and experience it as a coachee before coaching someone else.
- Be flexible.

Advice for the coachee

'Absolutely none. In the hands of a good coach [coachees] don't need any. Giving advice goes against good coaching process and will prejudice the outcome. What you really want is for the coachee to just go along and see what happens.'

Final thoughts

Trust the process. Everyone would get some benefit from skilled coaching.

Authors' comments

The process described here is very loose and relies heavily upon the facilitation and communication skills of the coach. These must be highly developed in order to underpin the confidence needed for the coach to 'go with the flow'.

Metropolitan Police recruits

Steve Taylor

Background and situation

Steve Taylor is a police sergeant working at the Metropolitan Police Recruit Training School at Hendon, London. His team has designed the Recruit Foundation Course there. The team also supports the delivery of that course and designs learning resources. Steve offers coaching to students who are on the 18-week recruit training programme run at the school. Coaching is usually triggered by the student, who requests it via voluntary study clubs, run on one evening per week

The coaching was introduced to support the formal training programme, by giving students access to staff other than their instructors, and was partly a result of a high failure rate amongst new recruits.

The process

Coaching is offered via informal 'drop in' study groups; it is usual for students to attend, certainly for the first time, at the 'failure point' – ie either they have failed one or more of their exams or that they are concerned about their ability to achieve the required standards. The students often describe the problem as not being able to pass the exams; in reality the issue is usually around how they study.

Once a student selects to attend the study group, Steve (or one of the team) coaches them on a one-to-one basis. This discussion follows a systematic pattern:

- Describing the difficulties and their symptoms. Steve encourages the student to talk to him about what the difficulties are and what the student feels is wrong. He asks the student to describe the symptoms as well as what he or she does. This way Steve is able to diagnose the problems whilst understanding the student's perception. Steve believes that you have to work with both the real problem and the individual's perception of what is wrong.

- Summarizing. At this point, Steve summarizes the main points, as described by the coachee.
- Changing perceptions. This is about giving the student increased confidence and putting the problem into perspective. Steve asks the coachee to describe in detail how he or she studies. He then helps the student to draw out what he or she does well, so that the student is able to identify development areas in a more positive way rather than focusing on the negative. For example, changing the student's focus from 'I can't get more than 65 per cent' to 'I am comfortable with these subjects'.
- Identifying options. Different ways and approaches for completing the study are identified. Steve uses three techniques for helping this part of the process:
  - The sharing of personal experiences such as 'If I was doing this. . .' or 'I had a similar experience when. . .'.
  - Helping the student understand what learning is by linking to other learning experiences, eg how he or she learnt the alphabet.
  - Focusing on the self-checking stage of learning – what does the student do to check his or her learning as he or she studies?
- Implementing – ie the student goes away and does what he or she planned to do.

Positive aspects of this approach

Steve believes that the informal style of coaching works well; it is different from the general culture of the programme, which consists of a formally structured timetable of classes, practical group activities and examinations. There are no written records of the coaching sessions, which are held on a one-to-one basis and, therefore, there is no feedback to the student's tutors. This anonymity, coupled with the informality of approach, helps the student recruits feel safe enough to discuss their individual issues honestly and openly. The improvements in pass rates since this coaching began have proved that this different approach is working

Another key aspect is the fact that the students trigger the coaching, which means that they are committed to the process and are open to trying the ideas that are discussed.

Possibly the most important aspect of this approach is the focus on identifying what works for the individual student. The discussions are based on finding out about the individual's learning and working styles, so that these can be used to build study techniques and routines that really work for the individual. A common mistake made by students is that they try to study in groups, and this can force them into learning through a method that does not suit them. Steve helps them identify as individuals the right mode of study for themselves.

Steve and his team have a high degree of expertise in training and development; they know and understand the programme that the students are undertaking as they have written the curriculum, and have, individually and as a team, many years of experience in training. They consequently have strong beliefs and principles around the whole subject of learning.

Challenges faced

The main challenge for Steve's team is that some of the instructors and tutors on the training programme are less experienced than others and this means that students are sometimes given the wrong information or support. This can mean that some students feel uncertain about following the advice of their coach, for fear of being seen to contradict their trainer.

Top tips

- It is vital to build a relationship that has its foundation in trust.
- Coaches need to be selected; line managers (or course tutors in this case) are not automatically the best people to coach as there is a difference between coaching and supervision.
- It is important to 'get on side' with coachees and to relate to where they are at the time of meeting with them.
- Don't tell coachees what to do, offer solutions.
- It is important to check that the coachee is comfortable with you as the coach – both of you need to have the option to say that it is the wrong relationship and that it won't work for you.

Advice for the coachee

Be honest – tell your coach how it is. There are no stupid questions.

Authors' comments

This case study highlights the importance of having an informal and comfortable environment in which to build rapport. It also shows the importance of having experienced coaches who have both knowledge of the subject and a strong grounding in development. We particularly like the focus on the need to change perceptions – the implication that it is people's view of their reality that impacts their performance.

Coaching a youth football team

Norman King

Background and situation

Norman King coaches a youth soccer team of boys under 14 years old. Professionally he is the Client Services Director for International Financial Data Services, and he has used his learning from the football environment to help him improve the way he coaches his staff at work. Norman's formal training as a coach was on an FA Coaches course; he has also learnt from doing it and watching other coaches, including those who have coached him.

Football coaching is an excellent example of a situation when you are concerned with the overall performance of a team; the coaching of individuals is based on getting each to improve his or her performance in order to achieve the team's targets.

The process

Norman describes the process he follows as a stepped approach, focusing on developing basic skills such as ball control, passing etc. He starts with the basics and then gradually increases the degree of difficulty, trying to improve each boy's performance without making it so difficult that he loses heart.

The coaching takes place during practice, where the team will participate in different exercises and tasks, after which they will receive feedback on how they have performed. He also uses the actual games as an opportunity to observe their play and review the team's performance.

Positive aspects of this approach

The advantage of using simulated exercises followed by 'doing it for real' means that the boys have a better understanding of the context in which they need to use their skills. Being able to relate their learning to reality and match situations resulted in a deeper understanding of what they were doing and why; consequently their performance improved.

Challenges faced

Norman's challenges in coaching the football team were about getting to know the individuals – who would respond to encouragement, who could take criticism. Some members of the team have learning difficulties, so Norman had to find ways of explaining the same thing in several ways and be sure that the messages the boys heard were the messages he intended to communicate.

Learning

- Keep it simple.
- Plan and prepare sessions.
- Don't tolerate non-triers – everyone can have a go, and to learn they must try something.
- The enthusiasm and positive attitude of the coach transmits to the coachee; it is therefore very important to display these attributes.

Top tips

- Watch the experts.
- Plan and prepare your sessions.
- Be positive and enthusiastic about your subject – this will transmit to your coachee.

Advice for the coachee

- Ask questions if you are not sure.
- Practise in real situations
- Be committed.

Authors' comments

Coaching is coaching, regardless of the environment in which it operates. A similar process can be followed in coaching people to improve performance in business, sport or hobbies.

Coaching two general managers

Jennifer Lindley

Background and situation

Jennifer was asked to coach two general managers within the same company. There was conflict between them ('they loathed each other') and this was causing problems within the company. Mainly, these managers were using their workforce to score points off each other, and this in turn was creating a blame culture. If a member of staff made a mistake, the manager concerned would not admit that the person had not been trained, but just bellow at the person for getting it wrong.

The process

Jennifer used the GROW model of coaching – goal, reality, options, will to succeed. For further information on the GROW model, refer to John Whitmore's book *Coaching for Performance* – (details in the Further Reading section).

Positive aspects of this approach

Jennifer was able to use the approach to work with the two managers individually so that they were able to see the impact of their behaviour.

Challenges faced

Jennifer was faced with the challenge of being a female coach within a macho male environment. She was frequently told that she didn't really know what these guys were like and that she was too soft etc. It was only when the managers saw the results of their changed behaviour that they began to come round to her ideas.

Learning

Jennifer learnt that sometimes clients are not ready or do not want to be coached. Building up rapport, credibility and relationships is paramount, but takes time. However, in order to make a permanent change, it can't be short-circuited.

Top tips

Jennifer recommends that people who are going to coach others should:

● work on their interpersonal skills – NLP helps;
● improve questioning and listening skills;
● find themselves a good coach!
● develop their assertiveness skills.

Advice for the coachee

Be open to new ideas and stick with it. Don't look for easy solutions from the coach, but work on your own solutions. And this takes time, so don't expect miracles too soon. Have faith, it works!

Coaching on customer service/ other one-to-one communication

Andrew Rea

Background and situation

In his work within the financial services industry, and subsequently as a freelance consultant, Andrew has been asked to coach a number of individuals around the issues of improving customer service and face-to-face communication skills. As a trainer Andrew had previously run training courses on coaching skills and was able to implement these skills himself when coaching others.

The process

Andrew describes a process called 'the fly on the wall'. This activity involves asking coachees to look at a situation from a number of perspectives:

- Their own – what did they see/hear/feel?
- The other person's – what did they think that the other person saw/ heard/felt?
- A third party observing – if you were me, observing the situation, what advice would you give to improve it next time?

Positive aspects of this approach

Andrew found that the positive aspect of using this process was that asking the learner to see things from another point of view enables them to get a different perspective on the situation.

Challenges faced

The challenges in using the process come when the coachee says, 'I don't know what someone else would feel'. To deal with this Andrew uses the statement, 'Imagine you do know' and has found this to be effective in 90 per cent of cases.

Learning

From this experience, Andrew felt he had learnt that most people are willing to change if they can see a reason why they should.

Top tips

Use questions, make it natural.

Final words

Andrew made a final observation on an organization with which he had an association – a large banking organization that introduced quarterly staff questionnaires as part of their 'balanced scorecard' measuring system. They regularly included questions such as 'How often do you receive coaching from your line manager?' or 'How good is your team leader at coaching?'.

The organization was surprised to find that the results did not seem to stack up, ie the staff in areas that were thought to have the best results and the best managers reported that they did not get 'coached'. On closer investigation the organization discovered that these managers were, in fact, so good at coaching that it had become a part of their everyday activity and therefore staff did not realize that they were being coached.

Subsequent surveys included questions such as 'How helpful is your manager? or 'How much interest does your team leader show in your development?'. The scores improved considerably for the better areas within the organization.

Authors' comments

This case study illustrates that coaching does not need to be a lengthy process and that using a simple, planned activity can have a profound impact upon the performance of an individual.

Andrew's final note gives an excellent example of managers who adopt a coaching style as their way of managing their teams. This style can evolve from using the more formal coaching process that we suggest here; alternatively the managers in this scenario may find that, in some situations, they use the process so that individuals can identify that they are being coached in a specific area of their work.

Coaching different individuals in different areas

Anne Cannings

Background and situation

Working within the aerospace industry, Anne Cannings had a number of opportunities to use her coaching skills. In this case study she describes three situations where she adopted different approaches and faced different challenges.

- Example 1. Coaching managers to use coaching skills.
- Example 2. Coaching a colleague in training delivery skills.
- Example 3. Coaching an individual through a career change.

Anne learnt her coaching skills by working with and being coached by others who are skilled at coaching. She also read around the subject, shared ideas and experiences with others. In the very early days of providing coaching, Anne participated in formal counselling training which established the key listening and questioning skills that she would use in coaching situations.

The process

- Example 1. In this situation, Anne implemented a coaching plan which was a combination of:
  - Skills exercises to show the effect of quality listening, questioning and feedback skills.
  - Feedback from others on the managers' performance before and after skills development.
  - The GROW model (goal, reality, options, will to succeed).

  By using this range of activities, Anne was able to model some of the coaching skills and techniques that she was supporting the managers to develop.

- Example 2. In coaching her colleague, Anne used a process of self-review and feedback from the coach immediately following a situation. This was followed up with action planning one or two points to work on (both positive and negative) in the immediate timescale. She supported her colleague to implement these points by providing opportunities to try the ideas generated as soon as possible.
- Example 3. Anne felt that, in coaching an individual through a career change, her coaching role was significantly different as it involved an expert, advisor role as well as the requirement for using coaching skills. In this situation, Anne adopted a change-based approach based on three areas:
  - Dissatisfaction – looking at what areas in the individual's career he or she was dissatisfied with.
  - Vision – considering what the individual would look for in any future career – not necessarily the job title, but the features of the job, working environment etc.
  - Steps – action planning the steps that the individual would take in order to achieve the vision.

This process was led by the coachee, who decided the pace, frequency and content of the meetings, with Anne providing ideas on how to take an area forward once the coachee indicated a willingness to proceed.

Positive aspects of these approaches

- Example 1. Managers were able to learn and accept that they do not need to have the 'answers' in order to help others to improve their performance – the answers can, and do, come from the individual. Additionally the managers learnt that the skill of coaching can be learnt by those for whom it was not their natural style or approach.
- Example 2. The approach used:
  - allowed the coachee and coach to discuss specific issues and areas of performance to be addressed directly, shortly after the event, meaning that the incidents were still fresh in both people's minds;
  - provided the coachee with the opportunity to quickly try again and implement suggestions;

- used very specific feedback where the coach and coachee worked on positives (repeating what works) and areas for improvement.
- Example 3. The coachee owned and drove this process. She took responsibility for the outcomes and this supported her in gaining confidence in the areas that she resolved.

Challenges faced

- Example 1. Anne found that the main challenges she faced in coaching managers to coach were around the perceptions of what coaching is and how it is done.
  - Some managers felt that developing others was not their role.
  - Some managers believed that by coaching others, they would undermine their own position, resulting in staff outperforming them, leaving etc.
  - Some managers considered that simply recommending a course of action, based upon their own experience/preference was coaching.
- Example 2. As a training professional, Anne found it challenging to work with how her coachee wanted to do things, resisting the urge to share what she would do.
- Example 3. Anne needed to be patient with the pace of the coachee. When she got 'stuck' at various points during the process, she needed to resist the urge here to tell the coachee what to do, thereby taking away the ownership that had been generated.

Learning

- Example 1.
  - Coaching skills can be learnt.
  - The coach should establish the coaching 'experience' that the coachee is expecting and use this to create ground rules, guidelines and the coaching 'contract'.
- Example 2. The coach should learn to ask, not tell. Anne believes that people's ideas, creativity and abilities will astound you and says 'what works for them may be different from what worked for you'.
- Example 3. Patience is one of the key qualities for a coach – the coach needs to be patient and allow the coachee to come to his or her insights when he or she is ready, even if the answer is obvious to the coach.

Top tips

- Seek feedback from those you coach and other experienced coaches to improve your skills.
- Don't be in a hurry to move the coachee on.
- Work with the coachee's goals not your own.
- Never accept that you have finished learning about coaching.
- Experience coaching as a coachee regularly to remember how it feels (good and bad).
- Remember to *ask* people what it is they find difficult/don't understand/ want to improve etc – ie let them drive the process or prioritize what is to be learnt.
- Never pull away from challenging performance levels.

Advice for the coachee

- Accept that the coach has ideas about how things can be different, but can't give you 'THE ANSWER'.
- Don't enter into coaching unless you are prepared to invest (time, energy, ideas).
- Tell your coach if and how the coaching relationship works/doesn't work for you – what does the coach do that helps or hinders?
- Say what is important to you.
- Remember that the coach should have your best interests at heart.

Final words

'Coaching isn't something you do by appointment, it's a way of working with people every day.'

Authors' comments

These three situations demonstrate that coaching can be adapted and used to meet a variety of different needs. They show how well the process can be adapted for individuals working in different situations.

Anne's comments reflect the relationship aspect of coaching and also the need for the coach to be willing to stretch the coachee so that he or she steps outside his or her 'comfort zone' – coaching is all about achieving potential, which can never happen until individuals are willing to accept that they can be more than they are at present.

Anne views coaching as a way of working every day. This reflects our comments that managers can adopt a coaching style within their work. This does not detract from the fact that there is also a process to coaching which managers can use and adapt to suit the situation.

Coaching an operational manager to take on a specialist HR role

Joce White

Background and situation

Joce was working as an HR manager within a large organization and took on the role of coaching an operational manager who was moving into a specialist HR role. Joce learnt coaching skills through her experience of being coached, from informal coaching situations and by learning from trial and error (trying different things). Her experience and formal training in group training techniques gave her a grounding in the knowledge and skills required to help others learn. Joce also feels that her natural management style is a facilitative and 'coaching' style. She has also picked up knowledge more recently by reading coaching books and applying the suggested models.

The process

The current skills, knowledge and experience of the individual were identified through an assessment centre process. These were then compared with those required for the new role. Together Joce and her coachee agreed a coaching plan, which took into account the learning style, personal situation, timescales required and resources available.

Positive aspects of this approach

The approach took advantage of the organizational culture where progression was encouraged. The organization was growing and there was a 'grow-your-own' mentality which supported learning and development. The coachee wanted to move into the specialist area and was highly focused and self-motivated – he was hungry for knowledge and was able to learn very quickly.

The coaching plan that was developed was based on building blocks. The coachee was not rushed and the process followed a logical order.

During the process Joce and the coachee were able to take advantage of real situations as they arose.

Challenges faced

Due to the time constraints experienced by both parties, Joce sometimes felt that it would be quicker to do certain tasks herself, rather than supporting her coachee to do them. There was some frustration when the coachee did not grasp things quickly and she needed to reassure him that, when things got tough, he should keep going and that she believed he could do it.

Learning

Joce found that coaching is very rewarding if the people involved are well chosen and the relationship works. She noted that a coach needs patience and the flexibility needed to take advantage of unplanned, 'real' coaching opportunities when they arise. Joce feels that it is important to inform colleagues and business partners what is happening, how it is taking place and why, so that if they are impacted by the coaching process, they will understand why. Finally she mentioned that 'there is no better feeling than seeing someone you have coached achieving what they set out to do and feeling great!'

Top tips

- Both people should be clear about what the coaching process is setting out to achieve.
- Agree responsibilities, remembering that these do not all belong to the coach.
- Ensure that both parties have the time required for the process to be effective and allocate regular coaching times in your diaries.
- Check that the coachee is 'hungry for it and 120 per cent committed'.
- Celebrate successes, however small.
- Be honest, but supportive.

Advice for the coachee

- Visualize what will happen, how long it will take and what is involved from you.
- Be sure what your goals are and that you are really committed to all that will be involved in achieving them.
- Ask yourself whether you have a good rapport with your coach and whether you can be honest with each other.

Final words

'Coaching happens naturally every day in most organizations, in small ways. Anyone who enjoys supporting others to achieve something that they want and has the patience to keep at it when things get tough, should find out more about "formal" coaching. In coaching situations, everyone wins, and feels great.'

Authors' comments

Joce's case study clearly projects the message that coaching has benefits for both parties involved. She has described some of the difficulties that coach and coachee will face because, in most instances, coaching is not the only thing that each person will be involved in, but she stresses that the rewards outweigh the challenges.

This case study also highlights the need to have a structured and manageable coaching plan that both parties have agreed to and are committed to. It also raises the point that commitment from the coachee will ensure that the process is very manageable and that results are achievable.

Coaching to expand the skills of an experienced trainer

Jonathan Smale

Background and situation

Jonathan was asked to coach an experienced 'soft skills' trainer to train on a management programme. The issue in this situation was that the coachee had the knowledge and skills required to do the job, but lacked the confidence to train managers.

He learnt how to coach from being coached himself – and had both positive and negative experiences of the process. He had also been involved in developing coaching skills programmes for managers and therefore had researched the subject in depth. On becoming a manager Jonathan had been required to coach his direct reports so that they would be able to take on increased responsibility.

The process

Jonathan used questioning to find out in what areas the coachee was not happy to deliver training and let her know that he would be there to support her. He used a process of asking her for her ideas about how to do things, rather than using a telling approach – he found that the coachee's ideas were 'spot on', ie they would be practical and would work. He followed up on the coachee's ideas with positive feedback and encouragement.

Positive aspects of this approach

Jonathan had been sure at the outset of the coaching that the individual had the necessary qualities to move into management training. The process itself gave the coachee the confidence boost that she needed.

Challenges faced

In his coaching role, Jonathan felt that the coachee wanted him to adopt a 'telling' approach, which he resisted. He found that his role was about teasing out the answers that the coachee already had. He needed to encourage the coachee to move out of her comfort zone – she would have been happy to observe him delivering the management training, but learnt much more from being coached to do it herself. Jonathan's challenge was to support and challenge the coachee to move beyond what she knew she could do, into areas that were unknown for her.

Learning

The coach should spend time in getting the balance right between telling the coachee and involving him or her in the activity. The coach should provide plenty of positive encouragement, especially when the coachee moves out of his or her comfort zone.

Top tips

'Don't feel that a coach needs to be expert or totally proficient in the subject matter. This might help gain credibility with the coachee, but coaching skills – such as getting the person to self-evaluate performance – are the more important qualities. Even Tiger Woods needs a coach!'

Advice for the coachee

'Be prepared to get into the "adventure zone" (ie not the comfort or danger zone) in order to fully learn. Reflect on your learning. Take and act on your coach's (and others') feedback – view it as a gift!'

Final words

'Every day there are coaching opportunities.'

Authors' comments

This case study has highlighted again the need for a coach to support his or her coachees as they leave their comfort zones. It has brought to light that there is a difference between an 'adventure zone' and a 'danger zone'.

Jonathan also highlights that the coach does not need to be an expert in the subject, but must have the skills and qualities to be able to draw out answers from his or her coachee and encourage the coachee to move forward. He also points out the importance of the coach having a belief in the coachee's abilities, from the very outset of the relationship. The coachee will tend to achieve what the coach believes he or she can.

Coaching a manager and a novice yacht crew

Colin Woodward

Background and situation

Colin was involved in coaching a manager through the process of terminating the employment of an under-performing member of staff. He also got involved in coaching a novice yacht crew to race competitively in a Fastnet race campaign. Colin learnt to coach through trial and error – he acknowledges that his own learning style is reflective and this has supported his learning by these methods. He has also attended some formal training courses.

The process

Colin adopted the same process for both situations and outlines it below:

- Understand the situation from the coachee's perspective and communicate your understanding in some way. This includes what the coachees want to get out of the situation, their motivations, needs, fears etc. It's important to ensure that the coach doesn't see this just as a training event – it's something that takes place in a wider context and the effect of the activity will have consequences.
- Identify the level of skill and underpinning knowledge that the coachee already has through some sensible questioning – sometimes it comes out of point 1 above. This helps to pitch the support at the right level, avoids being either patronizing or talking over the coachee's head. However, good questioning skills are sometimes needed in order to get past overconfidence or bluster.
- Assess whether you are the right person to be carrying this out – do you know enough or have the right level of skill(s) to do the subject justice?

- Consider how you can carry out the coaching activity – is it something that you can allow the coachee to do 'for real' straight away or do you need to role-play/practise in a 'safe' environment? (Safe means both physically and emotionally safe.)
- Take into account the coachee's learning style whenever possible. If this isn't apparent before starting, watch for evidence as you are coaching and adjust what you do as necessary.
- Think about whether the task needs to be broken down into smaller elements.
- Collect together what you need to carry out the activity and demonstrate the activity yourself – try to describe the experience as you carry it out, not just the bare facts.
- Let the coachee try it out for him- or herself, observe and provide honest but encouraging feedback that relates to the individual's needs. If 'good enough' is the standard, don't over-coach. However, if 'expert' status is needed then a more demanding approach may be required.
- Let the coachee 'own' ongoing development – offer support (if appropriate) but don't force it on the coachee.

Positive aspects of this approach

In the first example, Colin's coaching methods included role-play to enable the manager to practise focusing on the facts during the conversation with the member of staff. The timing of this role-play worked well – it was carried out immediately prior to the 'live' discussion and could be described as 'just-in-time' coaching. The process focused on the actual situation, not simply generic skill building. Colin was able to be present during the discussion with the member of staff, which helped the manager's confidence level because he knew that, if things should become awkward, help would be at hand.

In the second example, the coaching was more complex because there were eight coachees who all had vastly different backgrounds, skills and expectations. In addition the environment in which the coaching took place was physically threatening. The positive aspects of this coaching experience were that the group identified who would be best in which roles and established a set of core skills for each individual prior to widening their skill base, ie there was a gradual build up of skills and knowledge.

Challenges faced

In working with the manager there was a need to give this individual some background about employment law and the implications of getting the meeting wrong, without reducing the manager's confidence level so that the individual became a nervous wreck.

With the yacht crew it was difficult to give sufficient time and attention to each individual. This was overcome by using those who had grasped a subject quickly to support the development of others. In this situation feedback came, not only verbally from Colin, but also by participating in real races – this immediately made the crew aware of shortcomings in performance and, in early stages, did have a negative effect upon confidence levels. It was Colin's role to ensure that learning took place and these real experiences made it more obvious when improvements occurred.

Learning

Colin was reminded in working with the manager that what may seem mundane or commonplace to one person can be the 'equivalent of climbing Everest for the coachee'.

In the second example he felt that he learnt the importance of working on the coachee's expectations at an early stage.

Top tips

- Keep in touch with reality – it's imperative that you do the job/task for real.
- Don't be afraid to pull out if you are not confident of being able to do a good job.
- Understand the coachee as an individual and build the motivation to learn.
- Remain flexible.

Advice for the coachee

Give feedback on your level of understanding and confidence.

Final words

Coaching may well be the primary way in which the coachee is going to develop the skills and knowledge needed. Don't underestimate the value of it.

Authors' comments

This case study illustrates the way in which the same coaching process can be applied to vastly different situations. Colin applied his skills to an individual within an organization, and with a team brought together to achieve a competitive, physically challenging task.

Colin points out the importance of the coach putting him- or herself in the coachee's shoes so that he or she can view the situation from the coachee's perspective and thus offer effective support. He demonstrates that a coach, when working with a group of coachees, can use the skills developed within the group to support the process when the coach cannot work with everyone individually.

The case study also demonstrates the role of the coach in building coachee confidence to use the skills or knowledge that the coachee already has in different situations and new ways.

Colin mentions in his process the importance of allowing the coachee to own the process and the coach's role in identifying when the coaching has achieved its objectives – whether these objectives state that to be 'good enough' or that excellence is required.

Developing effective interpersonal skills in training

Leslie Rae

Background and situation

Leslie was involved in coaching a member of his Train the Trainers team in more effective interpersonal skills in training. This led the trainer involved to take over the existing interpersonal skills module and improve it where necessary. Leslie's coaching skills were built up through attendance on two formal coaching courses, being allocated coaching projects by his boss and being provided with follow-up support from the consultants who ran the training courses that he attended. He feels that much of his learning came from practical experience and learning from mistakes he made.

The process

The coaching was initiated by a discussion around the proposed future action with the member of staff, to agree a total approach.

The first step was for the trainer to attend three of the existing modules (three because in view of the type of event, every one can be different in approach and results). A report giving the trainer's views on the module was written and, again with agreement, a discussion took place with the module trainer, the coachee and Leslie as coach.

The next stage was for the trainer to attend an externally provided interpersonal skills course, run by a very experienced consultant of international standard. On return there was again a triad discussion, then the module trainer and the coachee met to agree possible changes, innovations etc. Both were given Leslie's go-ahead once agreement was reached.

The coachee held three modules, the first with the original trainer supporting actively, the second with the original trainer sitting in as observer, the third as a 'solo' effort. The coachee obtained validation and evaluation information and the triad met again to discuss the results. The coachee felt he needed further support, and attendance on a different external event was agreed and followed. During the next six months, during which the coachee was responsible for several module events, review dates had been agreed and followed with a final 'end of coaching assignment' triad meeting. The trainer then continued to be the trainer responsible for the module.

Positive aspects of this approach

The approach involved the generation of an open atmosphere between the three individuals involved. All members of the triad had the interest and enthusiasm for the project which led to an attitude of mutual support for the good of the module, the trainers and (above all) the learners who attended the events.

Challenges faced

The major challenge involved generating the openness required to achieve the coaching goals. This was achieved as described above, through the positive nature of those involved in the coaching relationship.

Learning

Leslie commented on the importance of developing openness within the coaching relationships.

Top tips

Learn as much as you can about the methods from books, open programmes etc; attend at least one well-recommended and experiential training course before you start to do anything. Then try to put as much coaching into action as possible, preferably with the support of a coach *in situ*, ie being coached as you practise coaching, taking simpler, easier projects to start with, then moving on to the more difficult and complex ones.

Final words

For the coach, coaching, performed effectively, is the most cost- and value-effective method of improving the skills of a person (ie training the person–the person learning); it uses work situations in the main and therefore is both productive while the coaching is proceeding and cost-effective without long absences on too many training and repeat training courses (other than those essential). But the coach must be effective in the skills of coaching, otherwise it is possible for more harm than good to result.

Authors' comments

This case study illustrates a situation where the coaching relationship involves three individuals. The description of the process indicates the importance of an effective working relationship in enabling the coaching goals to be achieved.

The process that was followed was a flexible one, initiated by the coach, but built wholly around the needs and progress of the coachee.

Leslie's comments highlight the relationship between coaching and training – the coachee attended two external courses to help with his skills development and the learning from these courses was supported and practised through the coaching process.

One-day breakthrough coaching

Julia Rai

Background and situation

Julia Rai is a qualified hypnotherapist and psychotherapist who is also trained in counselling. She is an NLP master practitioner and a Time Line Therapy master practitioner. She completed a coaching course for NLP practitioners with The Performance Partnership and uses a variety of skills and a basic coaching methodology which looks at values and beliefs, goals and achievable outcomes and has a practical, organizational element. This case study centres upon a 38-year-old management consultant who had been made redundant. She was finding it hard to find another job, even though she was very well-qualified and experienced. The coachee had become so depressed that she was taking anti-depressants. She decided she needed some help initially to come to terms with her fear and anxiety. Julia suggested a one-day breakthrough session and when she and the coachee met she realized that the individual did not seem congruent with getting another job like the ones she had had before. Julia suggested that they begin the coaching process by looking at the coachee's life purpose to see what she really wanted to do, what she was best at etc.

The process

Julia used various activities to support her coachee in analysing her personal values and reaching a conclusion about her life purpose. The first activity was an internal drive inventory; this involved Julia providing the coachee with a list of words or phrases – eg happiness, independence, being a leader – and the coachee explaining which words gave her a positive feeling. The words chosen were then grouped into key themes or patterns. Following on from this, Julia and the coachee went through some key stages in her life and looked at a key accomplishment at each age – one which had given the coachee the most joy. By exploring what was happening during these accomplishments they were able to draw out what the coachee really loved doing. An evaluation of the whole exercise allowed trends and themes to be identified.

Julia and the coachee then used a values exercise to find out which values were of most importance to the coachee. Having completed these exercises they worked together to discover some of the underlying issues for the coachee using a psychological approach involving NLP, Time Line Therapy and visualization – this work identified limiting beliefs and released some negative emotions.

Positive aspects of this approach

Julia comments that the approach uncovered some underlying personal issues for the coachee that were impacting upon her professional life. This is something that Julia finds happens regularly in this type of coaching. Coach and coachee were then able to work on these issues together, ie work on some of the causes rather than simply addressing symptoms.

Challenges faced

In this type of work, Julia finds that some coachees feel that their problems originate outside themselves and one of her roles is to encourage coachees to take responsibility for making changes within their lives. This process of supporting the individual to take this responsibility can be time consuming and challenging.

Learning

Julia comments that key skills and qualities for a coach in this situation are creativity and flexibility. Additionally she found that she needed to maintain empathy with the individual, even when she had some rather difficult messages to get across. Julia valued her own intuitions, which helped her to adapt her approach throughout this one-day session.

Top tips

- Get as much training and read as much as you can.
- Pay particular attention to goal setting.
- Choose a methodology that works for you before you work with others as you must practise what you preach.
- Demonstrate through your image and your way of working that you are successful – this will help others to believe that you will be able to support them in becoming more successful.
- Demonstrate your credibility within your particular area of specialism.

Advice for the coachee

- Take responsibility for your own success. A coach is someone who should challenge, support and encourage you but he or she can't make the changes for you.
- Be clear about what you want from your coach. Initially, you should have a goal in mind or a problem you want to resolve. As you work with your coach, other things may emerge that need to be addressed but initially, a clear outcome will help you both to get a good result.
- Do your homework! If your coach gives you tasking between sessions, make sure you do it. You are wasting your money if you don't do what you're told to do.
- Use your coach as a support. When you get downhearted or something knocks you back, call your coach and talk it through. Your coach is there to support you and keep you focused.
- Look out for sabotage by those who know you. When you begin to work on yourself, you sometimes find that people who know you start to see you change. They often have a natural tendency to want to pull you back to where you were. This makes them feel comfortable but may be detrimental to your progress. If you find some people begin to put you down or tell you you've changed for the worse, talk to your coach about how to deal with them.
- Be prepared for unexpected outcomes from coaching. You may find all kinds of areas of your life are affected by being coached, some you weren't even working on. Julia has had people find that the problem they have with work colleagues is also a problem they have with their children. Some people find the courage to cut ties with people who have not been good for them, sometimes husbands or wives.

Final words

Coaching changes lives. If you're not living the life you want to, coaching can help you get what you want for yourself. But be careful what you wish for! This is a powerful process and you should only begin it if you truly want to change your life.

Being a coach is a huge responsibility and you need to have integrity to be a good coach. You should also be able to walk away from someone you feel isn't ready for the changes that coaching can create. But it's great fun and highly rewarding.

Authors' comments

Julia works in the very specialized field of personal development coaching, but her comments and approach contain learning for all types of coach. Her comments around flexibility, empathy and creativity are important for us all, as are her comments about the power of coaching as a development method. Also significant is the fact that Julia mentions that some people around your coachee may try to sabotage the changes that the coachee is trying to make and also that coaching in one area of life may impact upon others.

Coachee in football

Robert King

The situation

Robert King has been coached by a variety of different football coaches, including his father, Norman.

The process

Coaching takes place during practice sessions – they begin with a warm up, followed by exercises aimed at working on ball skills. During the session, exercises gradually build up in terms of difficulty. The last part of the practice session is a 'conditioned' game, such as a game during which everyone has to touch the ball once. Some of the exercises are designed for a specific position.

Often, as well as explaining the exercises, the coach will demonstrate what needs to happen. Players are given feedback during and after the exercises.

Positive aspects of this approach

Robert thinks that the advantage of this approach is that the coaches demonstrate what has to be done – this makes it easier to carry out the tasks and focus on getting the exercise right rather than trying to understand the exercise itself. Given that football is a team game, being coached together enables each player to gain knowledge about the other positions.

Difficulties with the approach

Some of the exercises involve techniques that Robert has not fully grasped yet and therefore he is conscious that he is not always able to do the exercise properly.

Not all the players are involved in all the exercises, which means that often players have to stand about watching.

Top tips for coachees

- Prepare yourself before the coaching session.
- Listen to what the coach is telling you.
- Practice is good – you play the way you train.

Advice for the coach

- Plan what you want to do before the session.
- Be confident and clear in what you are trying to teach.
- Demonstrations are helpful.
- Try not to overcomplicate the sessions.

Being coached in project management

Jonathan Smale

The situation

Jonathan Smale received coaching when managing a project to introduce a computerized 360-degree feedback system into his organization. Initially Jonathan was given a free reign to manage the project. He received coaching only when it became clear that he was not managing the project in the way his manager would have done.

For Jonathan, this experience of coaching was poor. He received little direction or support in the early stages of his task, when he needed it, and the coaching only occurred once he was 'on a roll'. This led to him feeling a lot of resentment to his coach/line manager and had the effect of demotivating him.

Learning

Jonathan believes that despite the overall experience being negative, he learnt a lot about coaching from this experience, and specifically the importance of using a 'situational leadership' model of coaching. He thinks that not all coaching experiences require the same style and the approach that is used should be according to the situation and the individual being coached.

Top tips for coachees

Jonathan advises other coachees not to be afraid to challenge the coach or ask him or her questions. He thinks it is important to ask for direction and feedback as and when you need it.

Advice for the coach

Jonathan's overall advice for coaches is to ensure that the style you are using is the most appropriate for the situation and individual.

Being coached on specific beliefs/behaviour

Andrew Rea

The situation

Andrew Rea received coaching on his beliefs around time management and specifically about his habit of refusing help that was offered. The coaching focused on his effective learning – by uncovering his belief about the situation, he was able to change his behaviour permanently.

The process

The process followed was based on three-level questioning:

- What is the general situation?
- What did it come from?
- What does that say about you?

Positive aspects of this approach

It illustrates the power of appropriate and skilled questioning and listening techniques. By asking the right questions, all the attention is on the coachee.

Difficulties with the approach

Although an admirer of this approach to coaching, Andrew admits to feeling a little tense at the level of questioning.

Top tips for coachees

Having experienced and benefited from coaching, Andrew's advice to others who are going to be coached is that they have an open mind and let it happen.

Advice for the coach

And his advice to coaches? That there is always one more question that you can ask which will move your coachee on even further – don't be afraid to ask it! He suggests that coaches practise their questioning skills with a colleague by having an entire conversation made up only of questions.

Receiving on-the-job coaching

Anne Cannings

The situation

Anne Cannings was given on-the-job coaching by her line manager on how to manage clients and deliver client-focused events.

The process

Anne said, 'I'm sure there was a process, but it didn't feel like it – coaching was part of the way I was managed, not a separate exercise'. She recognizes that her coach used well-constructed feedback and questions, as well as providing her with opportunities to try new things.

Positive aspects of this approach

Being coached by her line manager in this way meant that Anne was able to look properly at how her performance was impacted by her actions, and explore how to make things better at her own pace. She was given plenty of opportunity to try new things, and her coaches showed complete trust in letting her carry these out. Anne felt totally supported in public, whilst receiving critical feedback in private.

Anne's experience shows that, if the line manager is skilled in coaching, this type of development can become an everyday way of working rather than an event.

Difficulties with the approach

Anne's main challenge was her own confidence to carry off some of the events she planned – she thinks this was mitigated by the confidence that her coach/line manager showed in her.

Top tips for coachees

Anne's top tip is to find as a coach a person that you respect. She would remind others that they will have to put a lot of themselves into the coaching experience in order for it to work.

Advice for the coach

- Drip feed is more effective than a downpour – employ the 'little and often rather than once in abundance' rule.
- Coaching involves learning and therefore has to go at the pace of the learner.
- Don't tell coachees what to do, help them work it out for themselves.

Life coaching

Jacky Rodwell

The situation

Jacky Rodwell is Managing Director of Central Learning Solutions. She received life coaching from Heather Waring of Waring Well.

The process

Most of the contact between Jacky and Heather was on the telephone. Jacky was given the opportunity to discuss changes in her situation and/or thinking. Her coach set tasks for her to complete between sessions; the tasks usually focused on getting Jacky to explore her thoughts on a subject and what she might see as solutions or other insights. These were then discussed during the next telephone conversation.

Positive aspects of this approach

For Jacky, it was beneficial to have someone who was distanced from her and her situation to talk to and who could offer her thought-provoking questions and suggestions. She was amazed that by having this relationship, she was able to see answers to her issues – she describes it as 'someone [turning] the light on'.

Although only halfway through the coaching programme at the time of writing the case study, Jacky could already see that she had most of the answers she needed, she just needed to learn how to search for them within. It is this that Heather helped her with.

Difficulties with this approach

The biggest challenge for Jacky was dealing with her own negative feelings and dealing with past hurts that inform her behaviour now.

Top tips for coachees

Be as open and honest as you can with your coach.

Advice for the coach

- Listen.
- Listen again.
- Ask questions.
- Do not offer solutions.

Overall thoughts

Coaching is an important, valuable process that can assist most people and most situations.

Being coached to take on a management role

Joce White

The situation

Joce White was coached by a non-executive director to take on the role of HR manager.

The process

The director was on a one-year contract and this imposed a timescale for the coaching programme. At the start of the process Joce worked with her coach to produce a list of all the tasks that she needed to be able to do; the pair then identified where she was and produced a plan of action. The coach then guided her, allowed her to practise, checked on her progress and gradually released her to take on the tasks alone.

Positive aspects of this approach

Because the director was only available one day each week, Joce did not rely on him and was therefore encouraged to work alone. The time constraints also meant that when together, the time was maximized. Because Joce trusted and respected the director the relationship worked well. He gave her positive encouragement and was honest with her when this was needed.

Challenges faced

Joce did get something wrong which could have been costly and damaging in her HR role. The challenge was overcome because the director was supportive and helped her to sort things out and analyse what happened so that she could learn from it.

Learning

Joce found the process of taking on the new role quite daunting – she was in the role and those people around her expected her to be fully competent immediately. Her coach rarely told her what to do and she was able to maintain responsibility for her own development. She suggests that a coachee should view the coach as a resource and that when a coach shares experiences and stories, these can support development and help to put things into context.

Top tips for coachees

- Want to do it for you; don't rely too heavily on the coach.
- Decide how best to use your time with the coach.
- Come up with your own ideas and answers, then discuss them with the coach.
- Keep reflecting back on what you have learnt and tell yourself 'well done'.

Advice for the coach

- Do it for them, not you.
- Do it because you enjoy it and want to give something back.
- Don't take over and control too much.
- Be available and flexible.
- Listen.

Part 3

Activities and exercises

Activities and exercises

This part of the book consists of a number of different activities and exercises that you may want to use in your coaching programmes. Feel free to adapt them and change them to fit your specific needs and situations. When you are using activities with your coachee, bear in mind the following guidelines:

- Only use activities that you feel comfortable with and which you can explain fully to your coachee. Read an activity fully to ensure that you understand it and try it out for yourself whenever you can.
- Use activities that relate to the purpose and objectives of the coaching programme or meeting. It may be tempting to try a new activity with the coachee because it sounds interesting to you – remember that coaching is about the coachee.
- The activities used should relate to the learning style of the coachee not the coaching style of the coach.
- Consider the time that is available to you and ensure that the activities chosen can be completed within this time.
- Do not force the coachee to do any activity that he or she does not feel happy with, but do encourage the coachee to try new and different activities. Be challenging, but not domineering.
- Do not allow the activity to take over the coaching meeting. One activity may take up a good proportion of your time with the coachee and it will be important to plan your sessions so that you can include reflection on the activity and action planning to apply learning as part of the process.
- Ensure that you always have the equipment you require available to you.
- Keep notes of when and how you have used these activities, what went well and what you would do differently next time.

Map your journey

Purpose

The purpose of this activity is to help coachees to:

- Identify their experience to date.
- Describe their goals or desired end position in detail.
- Consider what they will need to do to achieve their goals.

Resources

This will take approximately 40–60 minutes.
You will need coloured pens and paper.

Notes to the coach

This is a good exercise for the coachee to do prior to meeting with the coach, perhaps between Stages 1 and 2. Once the coachee has completed the activity, you can discuss his or her answers. Be prepared that the coachee might not be able to answer some of the questions and you may, therefore, need to explore why that is.

Instructions

Ask the coachee to sit quietly in a relaxed position and to spend a few minutes thinking generally about the skill or area that the coaching programme is concerned with.

When the coachee has done this, ask him or her to spend five minutes considering each of the following questions in depth, and to jot down on the paper any words or thoughts that come to mind. (It may be useful to explain that the coachee's notes are for personal use and therefore do not need to be 'neat' or in any particular format.)

Questions

- How well do I currently do this task or use this skill?
- How did I get to this point (training, experience)?
- Where would I like to be? Or what would I like to do?
- What or who is holding me back?
- How do I get to where I want to be?
- What resources do I need?
- What will it be like when I get there?

Highs and lows

Purpose

Use this to explore what has happened for the coachee prior to starting the coaching programme, in terms of his or her training and experience as well as peaks and troughs of performance.

Resources

This will take approximately 30–45 minutes.
You will need pens and paper.

Notes to the coach

The coachee could complete this exercise either before a coaching session or during it.

Instructions

Ask the coachee to draw a line from one side of a piece of paper to the other. This represents the passage of time from when the coachee first started the task (or skills) until now.

With a different coloured pen, ask the coachee to plot how he or she has felt about carrying out the task or using the skill during this time phase – positive thoughts and feelings should go above the line, negative ones below.

Once the coachee has done this, ask him or her to try to identify what happened at the times of peaks and troughs that may have caused his or her feelings.

Once the coachee has completed the activity, discuss the general pattern of the time line as well as why the coachee's confidence increased or decreased at certain times. Follow this up by identifying how the coachee can use the elements of the positive times when undertaking the task in the future. Part of this discussion will involve considering what needs to happen in order to keep the coachee above the line in the future. These actions can then be included on the action plan.

Example

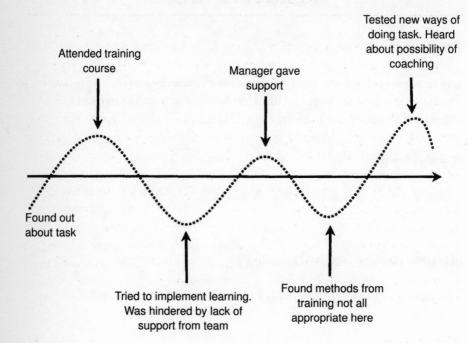

Spider charts

Spider charts provide a way of recording patterns of thought. Usually there is a central theme or idea that is written in the centre of a sheet of paper and the ensuing ideas are recorded around it. Ideas can be generated by brainstorming or gathering information about the central theme. Spider charts are also sometimes called splatter diagrams, branch diagrams or mind mapping (as created by Tony Buzan). This method is particularly useful if you wish to view all the information/thoughts about a topic on one sheet of paper.

Once all the ideas are committed to paper the coachee can then begin to link similar ideas by drawing a line between them or colour coding them. It is possible to further categorize the ideas by highlighting them in terms of priority, importance or impact. The level of categorization you ask for will depend upon your coachee and that person's general ability to consider his or her own performance – you may wish to do this part of the exercise together during one of your meetings.

Example

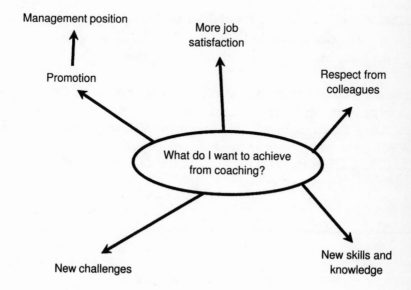

During the coaching process you may use spider charts as a method for helping the coachee to organize thoughts, reflect upon different areas or ideas and create action plans.

Examples of central themes for spider charts:

- What do I want to achieve from coaching?
- What is stopping me?
- What obstacles (blocks) and constraints are there?
- How do I improve?
- What do other people think about the way I perform?
- What is my ideal. . . ? (eg job, outcome)
- What does personal effectiveness look like in my current role?
- What do I want to remember about what I have read/learnt?

Categorization of data on a spider chart needs to be relevant to the subject and the specific objectives of the coaching programme. Consider the following ideas:

- Blocks/constraints that are real or imaginary.
- Actions that belong to the coachee or a third person.
- Things that are external or internal factors, eg feelings or resources available.
- Things that have happened and those that might happen.
- Items/activities/jobs/tasks I love, like, feel OK about or hate.
- What I do already or what I may do in the future.

Where the spider chart looks at a problem or issue area you could extend the activity by asking the coachee to build on the chart. Ask the coachee to take a different coloured pen and brainstorm potential solutions to each issue. This will assist with the creation of an action plan as well as giving you valuable insight into the areas that the coachee finds most challenging or is struggling with at the moment.

Force field analysis

Purpose

Developed by Kurt Lewin, this is a method for identifying how to get to the place that you want to be.

Resources

This will take approximately 40–60 minutes.
You will need coloured pens and paper.

Notes to the coach

In coaching, force field analysis can be used to identify how the coachee will achieve the desired end position. Once the coachee has identified the change that needs to take place, he or she can use this technique to detail those factors that will support the change and those that will prevent or hinder it from taking place. This process will feed into the action plan, in terms of helping the coachee identify the specific things that he or she needs to ensure happen.

Instructions

Explain to the coachee that force field analysis assumes that we are in a state of equilibrium, held in place by forces that are pushing in the opposing directions of for and against. When we want to make a change, we can map the opposing forces, review their various strengths and then decide which forces can be manipulated in order to make the change successful.

To create a force field analysis, ask the coachee to draw a line across the paper and to draw a different coloured arrow for each force pointing at the line. All the forces for change should be placed beneath the line, pointing upwards, as the direction of change is towards the top of the page. All the items that are against the change are placed above the line, pointing down. The length of the arrow will represent the relative strength of the force.

Example

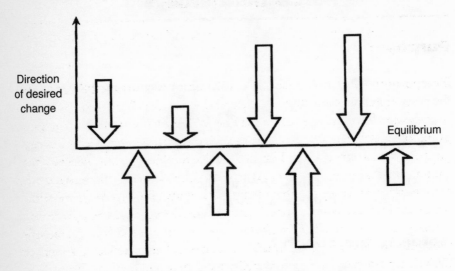

In order to make the change happen, the coachee will need to decide which forces he or she can alter and in what way. There are several options available to them:

- To increase the forces for the change – ie, make the arrows longer by increasing their strength.
- To decrease the forces against the change – ie, reduce their strength and diagrammatically reduce their length.
- Introduce new forces for the change, so that the line is pushed upwards in the direction of change.
- Take away the forces against the change, which means that the forces for it will take on increased power and push upwards.

Guided imagery

Purpose

The purpose of guided imagery is to 'put yourself into a different place without actually going there'. It can be used to reflect upon what has happened or on how the future may be. When used to reflect upon a past event, the coachee is able to relive the situation from either his or her own perspective or as an observer. This will involve recalling feelings, events, sights, sounds and thoughts. As a result of doing this, it brings these back into consciousness and they can then be used as the basis for discussion and action planning. Similarly, when visualizing the future, the coachee can use the same approach to picture what might happen – what are the sounds, feelings, thoughts, etc that he or she might experience. The coachee can then use this vision to discuss how current reality is different and how the future image might be achieved. If the coachee looks at the future and focuses on what might go wrong, it could help him or her become more motivated to make the changes. More often, this technique is used to view a future in which the coachee is being successful. Looking at the future in this way can help the coachee build a positive mental attitude and prepare him or her to move out of his or her comfort zone.

Resources

This will take approximately 20–30 minutes.
Music – if appropriate.

Notes to the coach

This activity may pull up some issues from the past that the coachee finds upsetting. You need to be prepared to help the coachee deal with this.

Some people find imagery difficult, especially if they are 'not visual'. To help this, you can change how you ask them to think about their past or future so that they are using words that appeal more to them, such as words relating to sounds, feelings or thoughts.

Instructions

Prepare a list of questions that will help the coachee to visualize in the way you want. For example:

● What will your life be like after you have achieved your desired end position?
● How does it feel?
● What can you see?
● What and who is near you?
● What can you smell?
● What was it like when you. . . ?
● How did it feel when you. . . ?
● What did you look like?
● What were you wearing?
● What did others say or how did they respond to you?

Ask the coachee to sit in a relaxed position, with eyes shut. You may or may not want to play quiet music in the background – instrumental music is best as words can interfere with the visualization. Encourage the coachee to put him- or herself into the required time period, future or past. Allow a few moments for the person to relax and picture the situation. Then begin to ask your questions, in a soft, calm voice. Allow a few minutes after each question for the coachee to visualize the answer. Sometimes, the coachee may want to answer the questions out loud, and if this is the case, you may want to record the answers so you can discuss them later. Other coachees will keep quiet and then be willing to discuss or write down what happened during the exercise.

After the guided imagery is finished, give the coachee a few minutes to come back to current time and gather his or her thoughts. You can then reflect upon what can be learnt from the activity.

Unfinished sentences

Purpose

This exercise helps the coachee to commit to a course of action by verbally finishing a sentence.

Resources

This will take approximately 15 minutes.
No equipment is required.

Notes to the coach

Below we give you some of the sentences that can be used to help a coachee commit to the action plan. However, this activity can be used with any sentence; for example, it is often used to evaluate a development activity. Make up your own sentences as appropriate.

Instructions

Tell the coachee that you are going to give the first part of a sentence and the coachee has to finish it with something that is true for him or her. Some sentences to use are:

- The first thing I am going to do after today is. . .
- I am going to ensure that. . .
- I will avoid. . .
- When I put my plan into action I am going to. . .
- I will. . .
- I will not. . .
- I must. . .
- I must not. . .
- I have to. . .

Tuning in to body language

Purpose

Either the coach or the coachee can do this activity. Its purpose is to help the individual tune in to his or her understanding of body language in order to improve his or her communication skills.

Resources

This will take approximately 40–60 minutes.
You will need a video recorder and TV. You will also need pen and paper.

Notes to the coach

You may want to do this prior to meeting your coachee for the first time, as part of your preparation. Alternatively, it may be a good activity for the coachee to do as part of the coaching plan.

Instructions

Video a short extract from a television drama or news programme. If possible try not to watch the programme whilst you are videoing it. Put the video on and watch it without any sound. Write down what you think the individuals in the video are displaying and/or communicating – what messages are they giving with their body language?

Now re-watch the video with the sound on. How correct were you with your original assessment of their feelings and thoughts?

Alternatives

If you and the coachee do this activity together, compare your notes; you may find that you have noticed different aspects of body language and/or interpreted it differently. If so, discuss why this may be.

Record a foreign film without any subtitles, and do the same exercise to review both body language and tone of voice. Be aware, however, that some gestures mean different things in different cultures. This activity can also work very well with animated films as body language and facial expressions are accentuated in this type of media.

Move your watch

Purpose

To look at how easy, or otherwise, it is to implement change.

Resources

This will take 10–15 minutes.
No equipment is required, other than the coachee's own watch.

Notes to the coach

This is a very quick activity that can illustrate to the coachee how uncomfortable it may be to make changes to his or her behaviour. It helps initiate a conversation about how to reduce the impact of change and how we can't always expect changes to our behaviour to feel right straight away.

Instructions

Ask the coachee to move his or her watch to the other wrist at the beginning of the meeting. After 10 minutes ask the coachee what time it is. Most coachees will automatically look at the wrist where their watch normally is. Later on, ask them how it feels to have the watch on the 'wrong arm' – this opens up a discussion about change and how it feels to make even a small change. You may find that your coachee moved the watch back after being asked the time, or has fiddled with it, showing some discomfort. These are all good points for discussion.

Give it back

Purpose

The purpose of this activity is to provide an opportunity to practise negotiation and influencing skills. It can also be used to help consider the effects of different behaviours, preferred communication styles and conflict management.

Resources

This lasts up to 30 minutes.
No equipment is required.

Notes to the coach

This activity involves you taking a possession that is valuable to the coachee, and refusing to give the item back until the coachee has used some 'magic words'. Generally the coachee will guess these words eventually, but you might need to be very patient. How the coachee deals with this exercise will be a topic for discussion and you may be able to relate it to his or her behaviour back in the work place or in certain circumstances.

Instructions

Ask the coachee to give you something of value to him or her, such as a watch, wallet or car keys. Tell the coachee that he or she can only have it back if he or she uses the 'magic words'. Explain that no physical contact is allowed! The magic words (which obviously you don't tell the coachee) are 'What do I need to do to get my x back?'. Note both how the coachee reacts to this as well as his or her strategies for getting the item back.

Once the coachee has got the item back, explore together why he or she did or said particular things, the impact it had on you and how it relates to the coachee's situation. Draw out the learning for inclusion in the action plan.

Skills checklist

Purpose

The aim of this checklist is for the coachee to assess his or her current performance and then to decide on priorities for development of his or her influencing skills.

Resources

Time required is about 10 minutes to complete the questionnaire and then approximately 20 minutes for discussion.
Copy of the questionnaire.

Notes for the coach

This activity is very good to use at both the analysis and evaluation stages of the coaching process. You need to create a list of skills relating to the area that the coachee wishes to improve, and create a questionnaire using a rating scale. The list of skills could come from a competency framework or job description; it could also be formulated following discussions with the coachee and his or her line manager. Consider using the same questionnaire at the end of the coaching programme to evaluate progress.

Instructions

Tell the coachee to rate his or her current performance in each of the areas noted. A possible rating scale is 1 = very effective, 2 = effective, 3 = not very effective.

Once the coachee has rated him- or herself against each skill, ask him or her to decide on three major priorities for the coaching programme.

SWOT analysis

Purpose

This simple tool is used to help identify strengths, weaknesses, opportunities and threats that exist for the coachee at any given time. It is therefore an ideal coaching exercise for helping the coachee plan how to achieve his or her desired outcomes.

Resources

This will take at least 60 minutes.
Flip-chart paper (or A3 sheets) and pens

Notes to coach

This exercise can be adapted to be used when looking at a specific project, or to review personal strengths and development areas. It can also be used by a coachee with his or her team to build group action plans.

Instructions

Explain to coachees the meaning of each letter: a strength is something that they are good at; a weakness is something that they find difficult or know they are not very good at; an opportunity is a situation that works in their favour or offers them the chance to move forward; a threat is something that will put their current position or future plans at risk.

Ask the coachee to brainstorm in each of the four areas and log each thought under the appropriate heading. If you have access to a flip chart encourage the coachee to use this, but make sure he or she removes and keeps the sheets when finished. Remember, the coachee needs to be honest and searching in his or her thinking, and to consider each area from every perspective.

Once this stage is complete, ask the coachee:

- What can you do to maximize your strengths and minimize the impact of your weaknesses?
- How can you take advantage of the opportunities?
- What can you do to overcome the threats?

'What if. . .' questions

Purpose

The purpose of this technique is to encourage the coachee to consider what might happen as a result of different scenarios.

Resources

This takes up to 25 minutes.
No equipment is required.

Notes to coach

There are many variations on this activity; it can be used to explore future possibilities for the coachee or to examine the consequences of actions. Your role as the coach is to encourage the coachee to think as deeply as possible about each 'what if. . .' scenario.

Instructions

When the coachee has identified a course of action, ask 'what if. . .' questions aimed at getting him or her to consider all the potential consequences that might happen as a result of his or her plans. This will help the coachee to be prepared for reactions to and results from the planned actions.

In the same way, use it to open up the coachee's mind to other options by asking questions like 'What if there were no limits?'.

Examples of 'what if. . .' questions are:

- What if you said. . . ?
- What if you had unlimited resources?
- What if there were no barriers placed in your way?
- What if you could do anything you wanted to in order to achieve your goal?
- What if you had different people around you?
- What if you only had a few months left to live?

- What if they say 'No'?
- What if they say 'Yes'?
- What if it goes wrong?
- What if you are successful?
- What if it isn't as good as you think it might be?
- What if your team responds badly?
- What if they tell you something you don't want to hear?
- What if you get angry?

Best in the world

Purpose

To help coachees identify role models or behaviour that will help them be successful in their chosen skill or task.

Resources

This will take approximately 15 minutes.
No equipment is required.

Notes to coach

Use this to help the coachee identify positive or good performance and behaviour traits.

Instructions

Ask the coachee to think about the person who is the best in the world at this task or skill (this may be a real or imaginary person). Ask the coachee to imagine watching that person do the task and to ask him- or herself the following questions:

- What can I see?
- What can I hear?
- What actions is the person taking?
- How are people responding to the person?

Use the answers to these questions to produce a list of behaviours and traits that the coachee wants to develop.

Cats and refrigerators

Purpose

To encourage creativity when looking at everyday situations and objects.

Resources

The time required is 5–10 minutes.
No equipment is required.

Notes to coach

This activity helps the coachee to use the right side of the brain, that is to awaken creativity. It is also a good activity to use if the coachee's energy level is dropping.

Instructions

Tell the coachee to think about the similarities between two unrelated but everyday objects and either write down or call out the ideas.

For example: the similarities between a cat and a refrigerator are: they both have tails (the wire leading up to the fridge), they both contain milk, they both have whiskers (mouldy food in the case of the fridge), they both purr, they can both be white, etc.

Other objects you could use are:

- a computer and a bed;
- spaghetti and tinsel;
- a handbag and a bath;
- a plastic cup and a window.

Alternatives

Ask the coachee to brainstorm similarities between his or her situation and, say, riding a bike – you could use any activity to make the comparison, such as: walking in the rain, having a baby, reading a book, making dinner, drinking brandy.

See Von Oech's book, *A Whack on the Side of the Head: How you can be more creative* – details in the Further reading section – for ideas on awakening creativity.

Evaluating progress

Purpose

To evaluate how close the coachee is to achieving his or her coaching objectives.

Resources

This will take 20–30 minutes.
You will need a list of the coaching objectives, pens and paper.

Notes to the coach

This is an activity which could be done prior to a coaching meeting or during it. The idea is to get the coachee's evaluation of how near he or she is to achieving each of the coaching objectives, which will help measure progress as well as inform a revision of the coaching plan if necessary. It is important that you allow the coachee to complete this without input from you as it should be his or her assessment of the progress, not yours. If you want to, you could undertake a similar review at the same time and compare your views with the coachee's.

Instructions

Provide the coachee with a list of the coaching objectives, plus the following three questions (if you want to, you could create this into a questionnaire or table format):

- How close to achieving each objective are you?
- What else do you need to do to fully achieve each objective?
- What actions do you intend to take now in order to ensure that you achieve each objective?

Discuss the evaluation with the coachee and amend the action plan as appropriate. You may also want to encourage the coachee to discuss progress with his or her line manager or any other stakeholders.

Review technique

Purpose

To evaluate actions, progress or the whole of the coaching programme as appropriate.

Resources

The amount of time depends on what is being evaluated.
You will need paper and pens.

Note to coach

This is a valuable tool for reviewing any activity including the total programme. Consider using it yourself for reviewing your own performance at the end of each coaching session or relationship.

Instructions

Divide a large sheet of paper into three columns. Label these columns from left to right as:
    What went well – How and why – Next time
Divide a second sheet of paper in the same way. This time, label the columns:
    What didn't go well – How and why – Next time
Working with the positives first, brainstorm all the parts of the activity or task that went well. After you have put all of them on the sheet, return to the top one and consider why and how the activity or task worked. In the third column write down what you would do to ensure it worked so well next time. Fill in these two columns for every item on your list.

Now brainstorm all the difficulties or things that didn't go well during the activity or task. Complete the columns as before. At the end of this, you will have a list of actions to do next time, which form the basis of your action plan for improvement.

My frustration journal

Purpose

The purpose of this activity is to record negative thinking patterns so that the coachee can analyse why he or she has felt negative at certain times. This then provides the information required for the coachee to turn the negative thinking around.

Resources

This will take approximately 15–30 minutes.
You will need pens and paper.

Notes to the coach

This is a good exercise for the coachee to do during the coaching programme and specifically as he or she tries to implement the action plan. It is fundamentally a reflection tool that helps the coachee recognize negative thinking patterns and identify where these patterns are coming from and the impact they have upon his or her feelings.

Instructions

Ask the coachee to sit quietly next time he or she feels depressed or angry and to let the mind wander. Once relaxed or calmed down, the coachee needs to ask him- or herself 'Why am I so angry?', 'What is really going on?'. The coachee needs to mentally review what is frustrating him or her and to identify whether it is fear, insecurity, regret, guilt or another emotion.

Ask the coachee to keep a journal of negative feelings, including recording the analysis of what led to the coachee feeling the way he or she did. When you review this within the coaching session, look at patterns or underlying messages that are affecting the coachee's behaviour or attitude to his or her work. Discuss how these can be altered or controlled.

Positive affirmation

Purpose

The coachee can use this technique to alter negative feelings or fears by increasing self-esteem and belief in his or her own ability.

Resources

This will take approximately 10 minutes.
No equipment is required.

Notes to the coach

This is a technique that you can share with the coachee so that he or she can use it whenever feeling unsure or believing that he or she cannot succeed – it is a form of 'self-talk'.

Instructions

Explain that whenever the coachee finds him- or herself thinking 'I can't do this' or putting him- or herself down, the coachee should:

- Stop.
- Create a positive statement of what he or she is going to do or the level of success – such as 'I can do this'; 'I have what it takes'; 'This will be the best . . .', 'I have done everything required'.
- Repeat the sentence three times, each time with more feeling and conviction.

Personality strengths

Purpose

To help the coachee identify his or her positive qualities and personal characteristics.

Resources

This will take approximately 10 minutes.
You will need a copy of the words given later in this exercise, and a pen.

Notes to the coach

We all have positive qualities within our personalities, but often do not take the time to identify them. This activity is a simple way of encouraging coachees to become aware of their positive qualities. It is important to encourage coachees to be as honest and objective as possible. A conversation about how they know they have these characteristics, or how they use them, may follow.

Instructions

Ask coachees to circle the words that relate to them. Ask them to think about how they see themselves, their personality, character, intellect and outlook on life. They can circle as many words as they want.

Accepting	Achieving	Active
Adventurous	Affectionate	Ambitious
Articulate	Assertive	Attractive
Caring	Charismatic	Charming
Cheerful	Committed	Compassionate
Confident	Congenial	Conscientious
Cooperative	Creative	Dedicated
Dependable	Determined	Disciplined
Distinctive	Dynamic	Efficient

Empathetic	Encouraging	Energetic
Enterprising	Entertaining	Enthusiastic
Expressive	Fair-minded	Friendly
Gentle	Genuine	Good-natured
Graceful	Helpful	Humorous
Happy	Imaginative	Independent
Insightful	Intelligent	Intuitive
Knowledgeable	Logical	Likeable
Open-minded	Optimistic	Objective
Organized	Orderly	Original
Outgoing	Patient	Perceptive
Persistent	Persuasive	Poised
Precise	Productive	Professional
Quick	Rational	Realistic
Receptive	Reassuring	Responsive
Self-aware	Self-confident	Sensitive
Serious	Sincere	Skilful
Sociable	Spontaneous	Steady
Stimulating	Strong	Sympathetic
Talented	Thoughtful	Tolerant
Trusting	Truthful	Unique
Unpretentious	Vigorous	Warm

Alternatives

This list of words could be used as a 360-degree feedback sheet – the coachee could ask his or her line manager and colleagues to mark the words that they think describe the coachee. A space could be included for the person giving the feedback to give an example. These observations can then be compared with the coachee's self-impression.

Edward de Bono's six thinking hats

Purpose

This method is a framework for thinking and can incorporate lateral thinking. Using this approach encourages the coachee to think wider and from a different perspective.

Resources

This exercise can take up to 60 minutes.
It requires no equipment.

Notes to the coach

The six hats represent six modes of thinking; the hats should be seen as indications of ways of thinking rather than as labels and should be used proactively rather than reactively.

The book, *Six Thinking Hats* (de Bono, 1985) is readily available and explains the system, although there have been some additions and changes to the execution of the method. There are also training courses that you can attend to learn how to use the method in a variety of situations. We are presenting you with a very short overview of the ideas here and recommend that you undertake some further reading prior to using the technique as it does require some skill as a facilitator to support the coachee as he or she 'changes hats'.

There are six metaphorical hats, which can be used to help the coachee think differently about the same issue or situation. You will ask the coachee to put on the different hats during the exercise – this putting on and taking off is essential.

Instructions

Explain to the coachee that you will be asking him or her to put on or take off a series of metaphorical coloured hats to indicate the type of thinking you want him or her to use. When you ask the coachee to don a certain colour of hat, he or she should try to review the subject of your conversation from this viewpoint.

White hat thinking

This covers facts, figures, information needs and gaps. Ask the coachee to wear this hat when you want him or her to view the situation in terms of the data available.

Red hat thinking

This hat covers intuition, feelings and emotions. The red hat allows the thinker to put forward an intuition without any need to justify it. We tend to only allow feelings and intuition to be introduced into a discussion if they are supported by logic. The red hat gives full permission to a coachee to put forward his or her feelings on the subject at the moment.

Black hat thinking

The black hat is the hat of judgment and caution, and as such is a most valuable hat. It is not in any sense an inferior or negative hat. The black hat is used to point out why a suggestion does not fit the facts, the available experience, the system in use, or the policy that is being followed. The black hat must always be logical. This mode of thinking is very useful for you to encourage within a coachee who wishes to try out new ideas that you feel may not be appropriate or effective for that person.

Yellow hat thinking

When wearing this hat the coachee must be logical and positive. The coachee should explain why he or she thinks something will work and why it will offer benefits. The yellow hat can be used in looking forward to the results of some proposed action, but can also be used to find something of value in what has already happened.

Green hat thinking

This is the hat of creativity, alternatives, proposals and what is interesting; it centres on provocations and changes. It can be used to help the coachee come up with options and ideas and can be used in conjunction with or following some of the creative thinking ideas also mentioned within this section.

Blue hat thinking

This is the overview or process-control hat and when thinking from this position the coachee can express what he or she think needs to happen at this time, eg 'Putting on my blue hat, I feel we should do some more green hat thinking at this point'.

Reframing

Purpose

This is a technique to help your coachee see things from a different perspective.

Resources

This technique requires 10–60 minutes, depending on the complexity of the situation that you are discussing.
It requires no equipment.

Notes to coach

It is drawn from NLP and further information on reframing can be gathered by reading about NLP techniques or attending a training programme.

A frame is the way we view a certain situation, activity, event or object. Each person has a different set of frames through which they look at the world. For example, a bride on her wedding day will view the prediction of rain very differently from a farmer who has just planted seedlings or a water company that has been experiencing a drought.

Reframing is seeing things through a different 'frame of reference'. It can be used with your coachee to help him or her take on different viewpoints and look for other reasons behind things and therefore to feel and behave differently if the same situation arises in the future. Use the activity when your coachee comes to you with a situation that he or she finds challenging. It can be used in conjunction with 'what if. . .?' questions or Edward de Bono's *Six Thinking Hats*.

Instructions

In this exercise, coachees are first asked to describe the situation to you – the facts of the situation, as they perceive them, the feelings that they are experiencing, the thoughts they have about the situation and the reactions of any others who are involved.

Then coachees are asked to think about the reasons behind their thoughts and feelings. The aim of this part of the activity is to help coachees identify the frame through which they are viewing the situation.

Having helped the coachees to identify their current frame, ask them to think about other frames that could be used. If coachees finds the situation frustrating, ask them what frame could be used to make it exciting. If coachees find the situation threatening, ask them to consider how to find opportunities within it.

Having found another frame to use, discuss with coachees what they would need to do to put this frame in place and how they will know when it is, ie what thought patterns will the coachees need to change and what parts of their behaviour might be different if they were to reframe the situation.

These statements of required changes can then feed into the action plan.

Using research

Purpose

At some points during the coaching process you will want coachees to gather information about a topic. The purpose of this is to help them review what they already know, find new ideas that they may wish to add, review the context of what they know and view things in a different way.

Resources

Research can take time, depending upon the depth that is required. Your coachee will need access to information. This can come from books, magazines, journals, the Internet, networking groups, managers, colleagues etc, depending on the topic.

Notes to coach

Some coachees will respond very well to being asked to find information for themselves, others will need you to be directive and either provide them with reading material or point them in the direction of a set of sources of information.

Instructions

With your coachee, decide what the topic and purpose of the research is. Discuss what the coachee can gain from carrying it out and how it will move the coachee towards his or her required outcomes.

Decide together the timescale for the research and arrange to meet to discuss what the coachee has found out. You may wish to ask your coachee to prepare a report or other written document about the research or to prepare a presentation for you. This will depend upon the purpose of the coaching, the time available and the learning preferences of the coachee.

At your meeting, discuss with the coachee what he or she learnt from researching and, more importantly, how he or she will implement this learning to help to achieve the coaching goals.

Encourage your coachee to note his or her learning and action plan and arrange how you will review whether or not the coachee has used the results of the research in a practical way.

Questions, questions, questions

Purpose

To encourage your coachee to think widely and deeply about a subject, issue, situation or problem.

Resources

Depending upon the depth of questioning involved and the discussion required, this activity will require 20–60 minutes.
No equipment is required.

Notes to coach

In order to be an effective coach, you will need to be able to use questioning skills and listening skills. Asking challenging and probing questions of your coachee will provide him or her with the opportunity to really consider his or her performance and how it might be improved in the future. Asking questions will come into every aspect of your coaching programme.

Instructions

Prepare a list of questions that you wish to ask your coachee about the topic in hand. Use open questions such as 'How. . . ?', 'Why. . . ?' and 'What. . . ?' to get the coachee to think widely about the issue. Use questions such as 'Which. . . ?', 'When. . . ?', 'Where. . . ?' and 'Who. . . ?' to get to the detail of the issue and then use closed questions such as 'Do. . . ?', 'Can. . . ?' and 'Will. . . ?' when you wish the coachee to commit to a course of action or when you want to ensure that he or she has fully stated an opinion about something.

If you are working with a problem, using a series of 'Why. . . ?' questions will help the coachee to get to the real crux of the problem. Once the coachee has reached this point, ask him or her a 'How. . . ?' question to help him or her begin to consider solutions.

A problem-solving process

Purpose

To offer the coachee a systematic process for solving a problem that he or she is experiencing.

Resources

This activity will take 30–90 minutes, depending upon the scope and depth of the problem.
Pens and paper will be required.

Notes to coach

In this activity, your role is to guide the coachee through the problem-solving process, not to solve the problem for the coachee. Your facilitation and questioning skills will support you in remaining objective, challenging the coachee to think widely and helping him or her to come up with creative solutions.

Instructions

Ask the coachee to work through the following questions relating to his or her problem:

- What exactly is the problem? What are the symptoms of the problem? How do I know the problem exists? Who and what does this problem impact upon?
- What is the cause of the problem? Are there several causes? Where did this problem first start? Who is involved? What is involved?
- What are the possible solutions to the problem? (At this point, encourage the coachee to go beyond his or her first few ideas for solutions and to be as creative as possible.)
- What will turn a *possible* solution into one that is acceptable and workable? What are the criteria for an acceptable solution?

- How do my *possible* solutions compare to the criteria for an acceptable solution?
- Which solution will I choose? Why?
- How will I implement this solution? Who will I need to consult with and work with to achieve the solution? What is my timescale? What resources will I need?
- How will I know if my solution has worked? How will I ensure that I learn from this process?

Once the coachee has worked through the questions with you, have the coachee commit his or her action plan to paper and arrange a time to meet in order to review how well the implementation of their solution went.

Questionnaires

Questionnaires can be used in coaching for a variety of reasons:

- to help the coachee analyse the coaching needs;
- to help the coachee understand his or her personality and its impact upon his or her performance;
- to help the coachee gather information about his or her impact upon others.

Choose the questionnaires that you use with your coachee carefully to ensure that they meet the requirements of the coaching programme. There are many questionnaires available, some of which must be administered and the results fed back by qualified individuals. If you wish to use psychometric tests and are not qualified to do so, contact the British Psychological Society who can provide a list of registered testers or details of appropriate training courses.

Some of the questionnaires and tests that we have found to be useful include (in no particular order):

- Insight Inventory (available from OTL, Worthing). This is a personality questionnaire that does not need to be administered by an individual who has completed psychometrics training. This test offers an individual profile and also has a 360-degree element to it to enable the coachee to gain feedback from colleagues and managers. The inventory highlights the differences between working and personal styles.
- Belbin Team Roles Inventory (available from Belbin Associates). This questionnaire provides information about the role that an individual will take when working within a team.
- Myers-Briggs Type Indicator (MBTI). This psychometric test must be used by a qualified person. The results of the questionnaire give an insight into where individuals like to focus their attention, the way they like to take in information, the way they like to decide and the kind of lifestyle they adopt.
- Personal Work Styles Questionnaire (available from Sherwood Publishing). This questionnaire can be used to identify whether your coachee prefers a 'Hurry Up', 'Try Hard', 'Be Perfect', 'Please People' or 'Be Strong' working style.

● Learning Styles Questionnaire (available from Peter Honey). This questionnaire enables your coachee to analyse his or her preferred learning style – activist, pragmatist, theorist or reflector.

Demonstrations

A demonstration is a presentation that illustrates a task, procedure or use of equipment, showing the coachee how to do it. It should always be followed by supervised practice. Demonstrations can be used to fulfil any objective to do with specific procedure, skill or behaviour.

In coaching, demonstrations should not be used to teach new skills or knowledge, but to illustrate either what the coachee did or how he or she could use existing knowledge and skills in a different way.

Preparing a demonstration

- Break the task or activity down into stages – 'bitesize chunks' – each stage being complete in itself.
- Plan to keep the demonstration short and simple, with as few key points as possible. Practise using slow movements to illustrate the points.
- Ensure that the steps demonstrated flow in a logical order – and that they will seem logical to the coachee.
- Check the objectives that your demonstration is designed to accomplish. Do the objectives relate simply to the 'how to' of the task or do they relate to the 'why' and 'when'.

Role-play

Role-play should be used with care. When coachees hear this term there can be a variety of reactions, many of which are not positive! Sometimes we substitute the word practice for the term role-play as this is more acceptable and feels less threatening.

Role-play is a powerful tool since it gives the coachee the opportunity to practise the skills required in a given situation without the 'dangers' of being in the real world.

Guidelines for using role-play

Generally you will discuss using this technique with the coachee and talk about the advantages of it as a method to support his or her development.

After the role-play, ask the coachee how it felt and what he or she would do differently next time – the review technique can be used effectively here.

You might want to consider getting the coachee to role-play with another person while you observe. If you choose this technique, the third party should be carefully selected and well-briefed.

Case study

A case study is a story about a situation or event relating to the objectives of the session or programme. It may be presented on paper, on video or using a personal narration. In coaching, a case study is a useful alternative to discussing the real-life experience of the coachee – this takes away some of the personal feelings about the situation and may prompt the coachee to think more objectively about it.

The purpose of a case study is to help your coachee to consider how he or she would respond in a certain situation and to put together a logical and objective response. The case study should be adapted so that it is as close to a real-life situation as possible, but so that actual incidents cannot be identified.

Questions to ask coachees when they are working on a case study include:

- What was the real issue in this situation?
- How could this situation have been prevented?
- How would you act in this situation?
- What can you learn from this situation to support you in your work?

In-tray exercises

This is a simulation which is an alternative to working on the coachee's own in-tray. The coachee is provided with a bundle of papers including letters, memos and telephone messages. He or she has to prioritize the papers and decide how to deal with each one.

In-tray exercises are time-consuming to prepare, but when used effectively can be a powerful learning tool. See the notes in Part 1 (Chapter 9) relating to using simulated experiences.

References

de Bono, E (1986) *The Six Thinking Hats*, Viking, London

Goleman, D (1999) *Working with Emotional Intelligence*, Bloomsbury, London

Gordon, W J J (1973) *Synetics: The development of creative capacity*, Harper & Row, New York

Kübler-Ross, E (1989) *On death and dying*, Routledge, London

Rogers, C (1967) *On Becoming a Person: a therapists view of psychotherapy*, Constable, London

Maslow, A H (1954) *Motivation and Personality*, Harper & Row, New York

Further reading

Alder, H (2001) *NLP: the new art and science of getting what you want*, Piatkus Books, London

Armstrong, M (1990) *How to Be an Even Better Manager*, Kogan Page, London

Back, K and K (1999) *Assertiveness at Work: A practical guide to handling awkward situations*, McGraw-Hill Education, London

Bentley, T (1994) *Facilitation: Providing opportunities for learning*, McGraw-Hill, London

Bloom B S (1964) *Taxonomy of Educational Objectives*, Longman Publishers, London

Buzan, T (1974, revised 1989) *Use Your Head*, BBC Publications, London

Cava, R (1999) *Dealing with Difficult People*, Piatkus Books, London

Eaton, J and Johnson, R (2001) *Coaching Successfully*, Essential Managers series, Dorling Kindersley, London

Goleman, D (1999) *Working with Emotional Intelligence*, Bloomsbury, London

Grant, R (1993) *Communicate with Confidence*, Mind Power series, Dorling Kindersley, London

Hardingham, A (1995) *Psychology for Trainers*, Training Essentials series, CIPD, London

Harrison R (2002) *Learning and Development*, CIPD, London

Hay, J (1993) *Working it Out at Work: Understanding attitudes and building relationships*, Sherwood Publishing, Watford

Keenan, K (1996) *Management Guide to Planning*, Ravette Publishing, West Sussex

Keenan, K (1996) *Management Guide to Understanding Behaviour*, Ravette Publishing, West Sussex

Landsberg, M (1996) *The Tao of Coaching: Boosting your effectiveness at work by inspiring and developing those around you*, HarperCollins, London

Matthews, S (1997) *Mentoring and Coaching*, Pitman Publishing, London

Mulligan, J and Human Potential Resource Group, University of Surrey (1988) *The Personal Management Handbook: How to make the most of your potential,* Sphere, London

O'Connor, J and Seymour, J (1994) *Training with NLP: Skills for managers, trainers and communicators,* Thorsons, London

O'Connor, J and Seymour, J (1995) *Introducing NLP: Psychological skills for understanding and influencing people,* The Aquarian Press, London

Parsloe, E (2001) *The Manager as Coach and Mentor,* Management Shapers series, CIPD, London

Pease, A (1984) *Body Language: How to read others' thoughts by their gestures,* Sheldon Press, London

Reay, D (1995) *The Complete Trainer's Toolkit,* Kogan Page, in association with OTSU Ltd, London

Reece, I and Walker, S (2000) *A Practical Guide to Teaching Training and Learning,* Business Education Publishers, Sunderland, Tyne and Wear

Robson, M and Beary, C (1995) *Facilitating,* Gower, London

Thorpe, S and Clifford, J (2000) *Dear Trainer: Dealing with difficult problems in training,* Kogan Page, London

Von Oech, R (1990) *A Whack on the Side of the Head: How you can be more creative,* Thorsons, London

Whiddett, S and Hollyforde, S (2000) *The Competencies Handbook,* CIPD, London

Whitmore, J (1996) *Coaching for Performance,* Nicholas Brealey Publishing Ltd

Zeus, P and Skiffington, S (2001) *The Complete Guide to Coaching at Work,* McGraw Hill, Australia

Skills

Analytical skills

Armstrong, M (1990) *How to Be an Even Better Manager,* Kogan Page, London

Assertiveness

Back, K and K (1999) *Assertiveness at Work: A practical guide to handling awkward situations,* McGraw-Hill Education, London

Hay, J (1993) *Working it Out at Work: Understanding attitudes and building relationships,* Sherwood Publishing, Watford

Mulligan, J and Human Potential Resource Group, University of Surrey (1988)

The Personal Management Handbook: How to make the most of your potential, Warner Books, London

Conflict management

Cava, R (1999) *Dealing with Difficult People,* Piatkus Books, London
Mulligan, J and Human Potential Resource Group, University of Surrey (1998) *The Personal Management Handbook: How to make the most of your potential,* Sphere, London
Thorpe, S and Clifford, J (2000) *Dear Trainer: Dealing with difficult problems in training,* Kogan Page, London

Facilitation

Bentley, T (1994) *Facilitation: Providing opportunities for learning,* McGraw Hill, London
Robson, M and Beary, C (1995) *Facilitating,* Gower, London

Influencing

Gillen, T (1999) *Agreed: Improve your powers of influence,* CIPD, London
Goleman, D (1999) *Working with Emotional Intelligence,* Bloomsbury, London

Listening

Armstrong, M (1990) *How to Be an Even Better Manager,* Kogan Page, London
Mulligan, J and Human Potential Resource Group, University of Surrey (1988) *The Personal Management Handbook: How to make the most of your potential,* Sphere, London

Observation

Reece, I and Walker, S (2000) *A Practical Guide to Teaching Training and Learning,* Business Education Publishers, Sunderland, Tyne and Wear

Planning and prioritization

Armstrong, M (1990) *How to Be an Even Better Manager*, Kogan Page, London
Keenan, K (1996) *Management Guide to Planning*, Ravette Publishing, West Sussex

Presenting ideas and information

Grant, R (1993) *Communicate with Confidence*, Mind power series, Dorling Kindersley, London

Questioning

Armstrong, M (1990) *How to Be an Even Better Manager*, Kogan Page, London

Rapport building

Alder, H (2001) *NLP: the new art and science of getting what you want*, Piatkus Books, London
Hardingham, A (1995) *Psychology for Trainers*, Training Essentials series, CIPD, London
O'Connor, J and Seymour, J (1994) *Training with NLP: Skills for managers, trainers and communicators*, Thorsons, London
O'Connor, J and Seymour, J (1995) *Introducing NLP: Psychological skills for understanding and influencing people*, The Aquarian Press, London

Using and interpreting non-verbal communication

Grant, R (1993) *Communicate with Confidence*, Mind Power series, Dorling Kindersley, London
Mulligan, J and Human Potential Resource Group, University of Surrey (1988) *The Personal Management Handbook: How to make the most of your potential*, Sphere, London
O'Connor, J and Seymour, J (1995) *Introducing NLP: Psychological skills for understanding and influencing people*, The Aquarian Press, London
Pease, A (1984) *Body Language: How to read others' thoughts by their gestures*, Sheldon Press, London

Index